BREAKING
IN**NO!**VATION
BARRIERS

BIS Publishers
Timorplein 46
1094 CC Amsterdam, The Netherlands
bis@bispublishers.com
www.bispublishers.com

Copyright © 2024 Gijs van Wulfen
and BIS Publishers.
www.gijsvanwulfen.com

Design
studio frederik de wal (www.frederikdewal.nl)

ISBN 978 90 636 9720 4

Gijs van Wulfen

BREAKING INNO!VATION BARRIERS

Fifteen Strategies to Win Management Buy-in for Change

BIS Publishers

Contents

NO

15 Strategies to Win Management Buy-in for Innovation 34-203

YES

15 Main Innovation Barriers

THE WALL OF INNOVATION BARRIERS

1 HISTORICAL SUCCESSES

6 ORGANISA-TIONAL SILOS

11 NO MARKET FOCUS

2 LACK OF DIVERSITY

7 RISK AVERSION

12 NO PRIORITY TO INNOVATE

3 FEAR OF FAILURE

8 RESISTANCE TO CHANGE

13 NO CLEAR DIRECTION TO INNOVATE

4 CULTURAL NORMS

9 SHORT-TERM FOCUS

14 NOT KNOWING HOW TO INNOVATE

5 BUREAUCRACY

10 NOT FITTING MANAGERS' GOALS

15 NO CLEAR INNOVATION ROI

15 Strategies to Win Management Buy-in to Innovation

CULTURE-RELATED	STRATEGY-RELATED	PROCESS-RELATED
1 UNDERSTAND YOUR MANAGEMENT'S AGENDA	**7** SEIZE THE INNOVATION SWEET SPOT	**12** APPLY PROVEN METHODS
2 CULTIVATE INNOVATION AMBASSADORS	**8** ALIGN INNOVATION TO STRATEGY	**13** PROVE CUSTOMER COMMITMENT
3 WE-NNOVATE ACROSS SILOS	**9** SHOWCASE INNOVATION SUCCESSES	**14** DRAFT AN INNOVATION BUSINESS CASE
4 ASSEMBLE A TOP TEAM	**10** FIND INNOVATION PARTNERS	**15** PITCH YOUR STORY
5 EXPERIMENT	**11** BE CUSTOMER-CENTRED	
6 BE A GREAT INNOVATOR		

Contents

Introduction

I was really fed up with being an innovator at my second job as a marketer in the food industry. Why? The organisation was performing badly; it appeared to be the worst-performing company in a holding of fourteen food companies. Top management was under tremendous pressure to improve profits in the short term and generate revenue growth in the long term. They urged us to create sales promotions to attain the ambitious sales target and, at the same time, drastically innovate our product portfolio to create tomorrow's cash cows.

So we ideated new concepts and, together with our research & development colleagues, presented them to our executives. But they turned us down. They rejected our innovation proposals three to four times in a row. Their arguments reflected their doubts about whether the new concepts would succeed. And we were sent back to do more research. This happened again and again. It was so... frustrating.

The only time we launched a new product quickly was when the executives were away on holiday! We did a kind of guerrilla launch. When they got back from their trips, we told the executives that we had introduced a new product to attain our sales budget for that year. And we asked for their forgiveness. They accepted our apologies, as the new concept sold like mad! Later, when I reflected on this turbulent period, I became aware that this resistance to innovation was fuelled by a pure fear of failure. A new product failure might have cost them their jobs as executives of the worst-performing company in the holding.

Transforming ideas into reality can be frustrating, not only for the innovators but also for your colleagues and other executives. Once upon a time, I met a CEO of a medium-sized family company. When started talking about innovation, he said to me: "Gijs, I have three problems with innovation:

> It always costs more than they promise.
> It always takes longer than they promise.
> It always generates less than they promise."

So, CEOs are frustrated too with innovation, and with innovators who overpromise and underdeliver. Did you know that 94 per cent of managers express dissatisfaction with their organisation's innovation performance? [1] Innovation performance is not about creating new ideas, although sometimes even that's a problem. For me, innovation means transforming ideas into reality and creating impact. And the impact of innovation can be anything: more revenue, 'wowing customers', more sustainability, increasing health. But it can also create social impact: making this world a better place to live and work for many.

I have made all the innovation mistakes myself. Later in my career, I created effective methodologies that double innovation effectiveness. My mission is to help you on your way to becoming a fantastic innovator. Travelling the world, keynoting on design thinking innovation, I meet many innovators from many different backgrounds and cultures. And it always strikes me that innovators are still frustrated and blocked by the same barriers in every sector all over the world.

That's why I wrote this book. To identify once and for all the main barriers to innovation. And to come up with fifteen practical strategies to tackle them. Pick the right moment and use them to become a more effective innovator.

Let's innovate and make this world a better place to live and work!

Innovative regards,
Gijs van Wulfen

P.S. A thousand thanks to Frederik de Wal, the designer of this wonderful book, Laura Woolthuis, the editor, and Harm van Kessel, the publisher of BIS. Thanks to you, thousands of innovators all over the world will break innovation barriers.

P.P.S. Maria Vittoria, this book is for you, amore xxx.

[1] Gitnux.org. Innovation Statistics:
Market Report & Data, December 20, 2023,
by Jannik Lindner.

Gijs van Wulfen

"Innovation
at the first NO.
moment it

doesn't stop
That's the
starts!"

The Struggle Called Innovation

When the change outside your organisation outsprints the change inside your organisation, you run the risk of becoming irrelevant one day. This is precisely reflected in research on the average lifespan of a company on the S&P 500, the index of the 500 leading publicly traded companies in the USA. The average lifespan decreased dramatically from 61 years in 1958 to just 18 years. It emphasises the importance of innovation, as many of these companies went out of business because they failed to make essential changes in time. [1]

Innovation Defined

Most people associate innovation with new technologies like artificial intelligence, biotechnology, and robotics. In business, however, innovation is related to new product development.

I like to define innovation more broadly, as I see a lot of innovation happening beyond technology and even beyond business in organisational, social, and sustainable contexts. Of course, the outcome can be a new product, service, or business model. Beyond that, it can also be a new process, experience, or way of working.

Innovation stands for 'transforming new ideas into reality with impact'.

Let me explain. Ideating is about creating new ideas. Invention is about creating new things. Innovation is applied ideation or applied invention. It means that your latest idea or new thing has a real impact. The impact of innovation might be qualitatively impactful, as it might massively change the way people think, act, or work. The effect of innovation might be impactful in a quantitative way, meaning the number of people, businesses, or organisations adopting it is enormous. And, of course, the impact could be both qualitative AND quantitative. There are new contexts where innovation started to play a more significant role than it used to. I like to highlight organisational and social innovation.

Due to a scarce labour market, attracting and keeping the right employees has become a challenge for many organisations. Younger generations especially love to work in a corporate environment where their creativity and entrepreneurship are stimulated, seen, and rewarded. That's why investing in organisational innovation makes sense. It helps create a great place to work and increases the loyalty of young employees.

More and more organisations use the ESG framework to evaluate their sustainability and ethical impact. ESG stands for Environmental, Social, and Governance. It has gained popularity as investors prioritise responsible investments and customers demand socially conscious products and services. Innovation helps organisations reach their ESG targets and create a positive societal impact by creating new sustainable practices, improving diversity and inclusion, and enhancing corporate governance.

Innovation usually involves departments like strategy, R&D, production, and marketing. However, with organisational and social innovation, human resources managers have also become innovators. One of the Innovation Stories will highlight the innovation journey of SEA, the Milanese airports of Malpensa and Linate in Italy, on diversity and inclusiveness.

There Are a Lot of Reasons to Innovate
Innovation rose as a top corporate priority, with 79 per cent of companies ranking it among their top three goals. [2] Great news, isn't it? Besides the continuity of an organisation, there are many other reasons you might innovate, too. I will list ten of them here. And you probably can come up with even more.

Ten Reasons to Innovate

There are many reasons to innovate, which is both obvious and surprising.
I would like to share ten reasons to innovate.

1. the needs and wants of your main customers are changing.
2. new technologies are emerging.
3. new regulations might force you to.
4. you want to create a culture of innovation.
5. you want to explore new business models.
6. you want to develop radically new products and services.
7. you want to make your organisation a great place to work.
8. you want to explore new target groups and markets.
9. you want to grow your business.
10. you would like to fulfil your ESG responsibilities.

And with all possible reasons for innovation in mind, every CEO knows that innovation is the key to safeguarding the company's future. McKinsey discovered that companies that harness the essentials of innovation see a substantial performance edge that separates them from others. Mastering innovation can generate an economic profit that is 2.4 times higher than that of other players. [3] Innovation leads to business success. It's as simple as that.

Nevertheless, for all the good reasons, practice shows us that striking a good balance between operational excellence and fostering a culture of innovation is a complex dilemma for many senior managers.

Becoming Innovative Is a Struggle

All organisations were once start-ups, too. And the 'old elephant' had become slow and stale when it grew old and big. It's a natural process that happens automatically. This means that in practice, 'focus on the basics' is a priority, especially in bad economic weather. In the end, "The business of today beats innovation for tomorrow", as I like to say in my keynotes. So, when you take the initiative to innovate your organisation, you're immediately confronted with the biggest obstacle to innovation: the word no! And as you can see, you might get quite a lot of different nos. You must recognise a few of them.

The single biggest obstacle to innovation is the word: no!

NONONONONONO

1. it's impossible.
2. it has no priority.
3. we've tried that before.
4. we don't have time for this.
5. our customers won't like it.
6. it doesn't fit the strategy.
7. the CEO will never say yes to this.
8. it's not in the budget.
9. it's not my responsibility.
10. it takes too long.
11. there's no business model.
12. we have always done it this way.
13. that's way too risky.
14. it doesn't fit our SAP system.
15. No!

No Management Support Kills Innovation

Although most managers claim they want to innovate, the majority wait until they need to innovate to adapt quickly to rapidly evolving markets and technological landscapes. In most cases, they prefer incremental innovation – making gradual improvements to existing offerings – over radical innovation, which pushes their boundaries and pursues ground-breaking ideas.

Recent statistics teach us that 94 per cent of managers express dissatisfaction with their organisation's innovation performance. [4] This reflects an enormous gap between the importance placed on innovation and the actual successful execution of it. And despite new ways of innovating, like open innovation platforms, hackathons, internal innovation incubators, big data, and artificial intelligence, there is no evidence yet that the success rate of innovation is improving.

Recently, I initiated a poll among business professionals asking them why innovation gets killed. As you can see, in more than half of the cases, it was due to a lack of management support. Surprisingly, a lack of technical feasibility was the least important factor.

What's the main reason innovation gets killed?

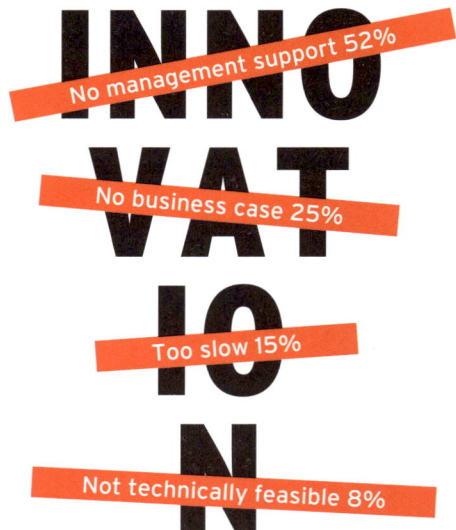

INNOVATION

No management support 52%

No business case 25%

Too slow 15%

Not technically feasible 8%

Source:
790 business profes-
sionals, LinkedIn, 2023.

So, to put it straight, here's the struggle called innovation:

1. *Managers all know innovation is essential.*
2. *Managers all claim they prioritise innovation.*
3. *But they're all dissatisfied with our innovation performance.*
4. *And when we start innovation, they kill it sooner or later.*

Lack of priority, senior management's dissatisfaction with innovation, and lack of support for innovation cause many struggles that innovation directors, managers, and project leaders face daily. Based on my impressions of them and conversations with them all over the world, I have compiled a list of fifteen practical struggles of innovators.

Fifteen Practical Struggles of Innovators

1. My innovation efforts are hitting a wall.
2. I have trouble getting innovation on the corporate agenda.
3. I struggle to secure a budget for innovation.
4. I lack support from senior management.
5. I meet innovation resistance from traditionalists.
6. I find it hard to foster a culture of innovation.
7. I run into bureaucratic hurdles with innovation.
8. I experience difficulties aligning innovation with strategy.
9. I face internal competition for innovation funding.
10. I deal with a risk-averse corporate culture.
11. I am frustrated by slow decision-making on innovation.
12. I encounter organisational silos hindering innovation.
13. I struggle to attract top talent for my innovation team.
14. I face scepticism about the ROI of our innovation efforts.
15. I face resistance to new ideas.

This book is a great choice if these struggles resonate with you. If not, give it to a colleague who is less fortunate than you.

Let's investigate why managers are blocking something they claim they really want, like innovation. In the next chapter, I will present the wall of barriers to innovation.

Key Messages from This Chapter:

☞ There are a lot of reasons to innovate.

☞ Senior managers claim to prioritise innovation. But rarely go through with it.

☞ The single biggest obstacle to innovation is the word: no!

☞ Management is dissatisfied with innovation performance.

☞ The main reason why innovation stops is that there is no management support.

[1] Innosight Report. https://www.innosight.com/wp-content/uploads/2016/08/creative-destruction-whips-through-corporate-america_final2015.pdf.
[2] BCG. https://media-publications.bcg.com/BCG_Most-Innovative-Companies-2023.
[3] *McKinsey Insights*. 'What is innovation?' August 17, 2022.
[4] Gitnux.org. Innovation Statistics: Market Report & Data, December 20, 2023, by Jannik Lindner.

Gijs van Wulfen

"The Business of Today beats Innovation for Tomorrow."

The Wall: Fifteen Main Barriers to Innovation

In my professional career as a marketer in the food industry, consultant, and innovation facilitator, I immersed myself entirely in the struggle known as innovation. I was frustrated by hearing all the nos, but I could not accept that agile start-ups repeatedly outperformed big organisations. That's why I left corporate life twenty years ago to create an innovation methodology to help 'old elephants to dance again'. And I succeeded, with much perseverance.

On a mission to help you become an amazing innovator, I teach the FORTH innovation method, train innovation facilitators, and inspire business professionals on big stages with my storytelling innovation keynotes from Tokyo to Madrid and from South Africa to Mexico.

Fifteen Significant Barriers to Innovation

And still, everywhere, I see innovators and managers struggling as I once did. Struggling to get innovation prioritised, to get resources, and to keep management support in the innovation funnel so new initiatives can be launched. I encountered, like you, many ways in which innovation was completely ignored, politically sabotaged, or suddenly stopped—mostly for vague reasons. Based on my vast experience in many sectors all over the world, I reflected on the obstacles to innovation. After several pivots, I identified fifteen barriers to innovation. I like to depict them as a wall of fifteen barriers to innovation that we must break through as innovators!

This wall contains fifteen significant barriers you might have experienced yourself, more than once in your career, working as a corporate innovator or start-up entrepreneur. And yes, of course, the barriers are interconnected. Most of the time, a lack of management buy-in for innovation stems from a combination of multiple factors. I like to explore them one by one and see how they resonate with you.

1. Historical successes: Organisations tend to rely on past achievements, leading to complacency. When a company has achieved success from a specific product or service in the past, there's often a great reluctance to deviate from these tried-and-true approaches, hindering innovation. For example, a technology company that has been producing and selling a particular type of successful software for years is mostly hesitant to explore new software solutions or innovative approaches, fearing that they might not replicate the same level of success. They only develop new versions and features of their old system. Especially in family companies, reliance on historical achievements can be very persistent.

15 Main Innovation Barriers

THE WALL OF INNOVATION BARRIERS

1 HISTORICAL SUCCESSES

2 LACK OF DIVERSITY

3 FEAR OF FAILURE

4 CULTURAL NORMS

5 BUREAUCRACY

6 ORGANISATIONAL SILOS

7 RISK AVERSION

8 RESISTANCE TO CHANGE

9 SHORT-TERM FOCUS

10 NOT FITTING MANAGERS' GOALS

11 NO MARKET FOCUS

12 NO PRIORITY TO INNOVATE

13 NO CLEAR DIRECTION TO INNOVATE

14 NOT KNOWING HOW TO INNOVATE

15 NO CLEAR INNOVATION ROI

2. Lack of diversity: Without diverse perspectives, backgrounds, and experiences within an organisation, innovation can be stifled. This is typically the case at conservative organisations with a strong corporate culture, like big law firms, financial institutions, or governmental organisations. For example, an innovation team that consists primarily of individuals from similar backgrounds and experiences leads to a lack of diverse perspectives when brainstorming new concepts. Without input from a diverse range of voices, innovation teams struggle to develop disruptive solutions, generating more and more incremental improvements.

3. Fear of failure: Fear of failure is a persistent, irrational fear of failing to achieve one's goals. It can paralyse individuals and organisations, preventing them from taking the risks necessary for innovation. A pharmaceutical company may be considering investing in research and development for a new drug, but the executives are hesitant to greenlight the project due to the high risk of failure associated with drug development. The fear of investing resources into a project that may yield unsuccessful results hinders an organisation's ability to pursue potentially groundbreaking innovations. They mostly stick to incremental innovation.

4. Cultural norms: Cultural norms within an organisation can either foster or hinder innovation. Cultures differ among countries and sectors. Cultures that prioritise hierarchy, conformity, and risk aversion - like Japan, for example -, may discourage creativity and hinder the free flow of ideas. There are also typical corporate cultural norms. For instance, a traditional big accountancy firm has a hierarchical culture where junior accountants are expected to follow established procedures and defer to senior partners. This culture discourages junior accountants from proposing new approaches or questioning existing practices, stifling innovation within the firm.

5. Bureaucracy: Bureaucratic processes and red tape can slow down decision-making and innovation within an organisation. Bureaucracy can be defined as a process without a purpose. Layers of bureaucracy can stifle creativity and make it difficult for innovative ideas to gain traction. For example, a government agency might require multiple approval levels for any new project or initiative, leading to lengthy bureaucratic processes. As a result, innovative ideas often fail to gain traction, discouraging employees from continuing to suggest something innovative ever again.

Ten Great Innovations Originally Rejected by Senior Decision Makers [1]

"This 'telephone' has too many shortcomings to be seriously considered as a means of communication. The device is inherently of no value to us."
– *Western Union internal memo, 1876.*

"I do not believe the introduction of motorcars will ever affect the riding of horses."
– *Mr. Scott-Montague, MP, United Kingdom, 1903.*

"The wireless music box has no imaginable commercial value. Who would pay for a message sent to nobody in particular?"
– *David Sarnoff's Associates rejecting a proposal for investment in the radio, the 1920s.*

"Who the hell wants to hear actors talk?"
H.M. Warner (Warner Brothers) before rejecting a proposal for movies with sound, 1927.

"This is typical Berlin hot air. The product is worthless."
– *Letter sent by Heinrich Dreser, head of Bayer's Pharmacological Institute, rejecting Felix Hoffmann's invention of aspirin.*

"Who the hell wants to copy a document on plain paper?"
Rejection letter in 1940 to Chester Carlson, inventor of the XEROX machine.

"The concept is interesting and well-formed, but in order to earn better than a 'C,' the idea must be feasible."
– *A Yale university professor in response to Fred Smith's paper proposing reliable overnight delivery service. Smith went on to found Federal Express.*

"There is no reason anyone would want a computer in their home."
– *Ken Olsen, President, Chairman and Founder of Digital Equipment Corp, 1977.*

"You want to have consistent and uniform muscle development across all of your muscles? It can't be done. It's just a fact of life."
– *Rejection letter to Arthur Jones, who invented the Nautilus Fitness Machine.*

6. Organisational silos: Siloed departments and a lack of communication between them inhibit innovation by preventing the sharing of ideas and resources. I experienced that in big organisations, departments might work on the same opportunities without knowing it. A large manufacturing company, for example, has separate departments for design, production, and marketing, with limited communication and collaboration. As a result, innovative product ideas generated by the design team are not effectively communicated to the production and marketing teams, hindering the development and launch of new products. Organisational silos suffer from the so-called 'not invented here' syndrome.

7. Risk aversion: Risk aversion is the tendency to avoid risk and have a low-risk tolerance. Large organisations especially tend to encourage bureaucracy and adaptation to minimise risk and attain a high degree of conformity. As a result, they are hesitant to invest in innovative ideas or ventures due to the perceived uncertainty. A financial institution might be hesitant to invest in emerging technologies such as blockchain or artificial intelligence due to the perceived risks associated with these technologies. Despite the potential benefits they could bring, the company's risk-averse culture prevents it from exploring innovative solutions that could enhance its financial services and operations.

8. Resistance to change: Human nature often resists change, and this resistance manifests within organisations, killing innovation. Middle managers often resist change because they focus more on getting things done quickly and achieving immediate results. As they are responsible for operational excellence, most middle managers trust present best practices, hesitating to try new ideas. They fear losing their jobs, so they rely on tested ways of getting things done. An established retail chain, for example, is resistant to implementing e-commerce solutions and digital payment options, preferring to stick with traditional brick-and-mortar stores. Despite the changing retail landscape and consumer preferences, the company's resistance to change hinders its ability to innovate and adapt quickly to new market trends.

9. Short-term focus: Focusing solely on short-term goals and immediate results detract from long-term innovation efforts. Big companies have a short-term focus because they face pressure from shareholders and the market to deliver immediate results. Stock-listed companies are especially eager to meet quarterly financial targets, which might overshadow their long-term strategic planning.

10. Not fitting managers' goals: When innovation initiatives do not align with the goals and priorities of upper management or key decision-makers, they may not receive the necessary support and resources. An employee might propose, for example, a new project aimed at developing a new line of sustainable packaging solutions, which will take three years after some considerable investment. However, this project does not align with upper management's priority of raising profits in the current year, leading to a lack of support and a denial of the necessary funding to start the new sustainable packaging initiative.

Five Main Innovation Barriers at a Bank in the Middle East

The banking industry has undergone significant changes over the last decades as innovations have enabled new digital banking services and created new customer mobile requirements. I would like to share with you a scientific case study of a Jordanian commercial bank to determine the key perceived barriers to change and innovation from the perspective of its senior management. [2]

A New Transformational Banking System

The bank is a significant bank with over 2,400 employees, 134 branches in Jordan, and 56 overseas branches. According to the study's interviewees, the bank implemented a new transformational banking system, and they recognised its positive outcomes and the radical transformation that occurred because of its implementation. They emphasised the importance of this system in helping the bank develop new products and services.

According to one manager: "The transformation was regarded as radical and stressful. This was a difficult period since changing the whole banking system was not easy. It was a transformative, dramatic shift."

Another senior manager said: "Every novel approach takes time to implement. For example, we spent a significant amount of time planning, marketing, and convincing people to use mobile banking... This system represents a complete shift in the bank and is seen as a means of changing the old mindsets of people using the previous system for more than twenty years..."

The study reports that senior management identified five barriers that stifled innovation and change: high bureaucracy, lack of communication and employee involvement, middle management resistance, and risk avoidance.
I would love to share more quotes highlighting some of these barriers with you.

Regarding the 'high bureaucracy', one manager said: "We have a significant number of rules and procedures to help us in our profession; we truly need them as workers since certain individuals are not mature enough to work independently. The bank's heavy bureaucracy inhibits many things that could have been changed; this slows down operations and occasionally stifles innovation. Nevertheless, those hierarchical processes and norms are critical in forcing people to accept innovations and deal with change correctly... since these procedures guide us through the innovation process."

The study reveals that involving employees in the change process from the beginning is critical. One manager stated: "I believe that for employees to accept changes smoothly, they must be involved in the change process from the start. There is an 80 per cent likelihood of project failure if employees do not accept the change. This is due to a lack of employee engagement when there is a misalignment between the change process and employees' involvement and awareness of the change."

Furthermore, it is interesting that the study emphasises the issue of managers' old mindsets and how this hampered innovation: "Some middle managers' beliefs were a barrier to change, operating according to old stereotypes and claiming, 'Why change; we are doing fine as we are.' A portion of middle managers always oppose change and argue that there is no need for change because they are accustomed to the same way of working."

On risk aversion, another manager stated: "The most important thing that must be done is to identify those risks and control them; however, some risks are known as residual risks, which you must accept in the business and deal with; otherwise, we cannot do business. All these technology-based new product innovations and trends must be given a significant amount of time before being released to the market, as they must be fully ready and secure."

This study was excellent exploratory research on barriers to innovation in a traditional sector undergoing a major change. All five barriers mentioned are reflected in some way in 'The Wall of Innovation Barriers,' which I present to you in this book.

----

11. No market focus: Innovation efforts that lack a clear understanding of market needs and customer preferences struggle to gain traction. An example is a big high-tech organisation introducing groundbreaking technology into a new wearable product containing new-to-the-world features that fail to gain adoption due to social acceptance issues and a lack of a clear value proposition for consumers.

12. No priority to innovate: In organisations where innovation is not prioritised or seen as a secondary concern, resources and support for innovation initiatives are limited. A manufacturing company might focus solely on increasing production efficiency and reducing costs, with little emphasis on innovation or product development. Without a strategic priority placed on innovation, the company misses out on opportunities to introduce new products or processes that could drive growth and competitiveness in the long term.

13. No clear direction to innovate: Organisations struggle to effectively channel their efforts and resources towards meaningful innovation initiatives without a clear vision and strategy for innovation. A high-technology company might encourage employees to be innovative but fail to provide clear guidelines or goals for innovation initiatives. As a result, employees feel uncertain about where to focus their efforts or how to measure success, leading to a lack of direction and alignment in their innovation efforts.

14. Not knowing how to innovate: Lack of knowledge or expertise in innovation processes and methodologies impedes organisations' ability to innovate effectively. A medium-sized business owner recognises the importance of innovation but lacks knowledge or expertise in innovation processes and methodologies. Without access to resources or know-how to innovate effectively, the business owner struggles to generate and implement innovative ideas to drive growth and competitiveness.

15. No clear innovation ROI (Return on Investment): Senior managers are hesitant to allocate resources to innovation initiatives without a clear understanding of the potential return on investment (ROI) of innovation efforts. A digital innovation team, for example, might invest resources in launching an advertising campaign for a new digital solution without a clear understanding of how to measure the return on investment. Without clear metrics or tracking mechanisms in place, the team struggles to evaluate the product launch's effectiveness and justify future investment in similar new digital initiatives.

I trust these fifteen barriers to innovation resonate well with you. All fifteen barriers, and even more, are common challenges faced by innovators in many organisations. But with awareness, proactive strategies, and a commitment to fostering a culture of innovation, you can overcome them to drive meaningful change and growth.

I will provide you with fifteen proven strategies for winning management buy-in for radical change, helping you overcome each of the barriers on your path to becoming an amazing innovator.

Key Messages from This Chapter:

☞ Significant innovations have been rejected throughout history.

☞ Innovators everywhere are hitting a wall of fifteen main barriers to innovation.

☞ All innovation barriers relate to the company's culture, the chosen strategy, or a lack of an innovation process.

[1] Greekchat.com. http://www.greekchat.com/gcforums/showthread.php?t=45503
[2] Alshwayat D., Elrehail H., Shehadeh E., Alsalhi N., Shamout M.D. & Rehman S.U., 'An Exploratory Examination of the Barriers to Innovation and Change as Perceived by Senior Management', *International Journal of Innovation Studies*, https://doi.org/10.1016/j.ijis.2022.12.005.

Peter Drucker

"Most managers
chosen for their
better instead
to do

have been
ability to do
of their courage
differently."

Fifteen Strategies to Win Management Buy-In for Change

All fifteen barriers to innovation I presented in the previous chapter, are common challenges faced by many innovators all over the world. In this chapter, I will explore fifteen proven practical strategies to break through these barriers and help you win the support you need from your senior managers to prioritise and drive innovation successfully.

Based on the struggle called innovation you, as innovator,

1. *Must remind your managers that innovation is essential.*
2. *Help your managers to prioritise innovation.*
3. *Satisfy your senior managers better with your innovation performance.*
4. *Win your managers' buy-in to keep your innovation projects alive and kicking.*

How? That's the main theme of this book. I wish I could provide you with one simple solution to end the innovation struggle. Unfortunately, there isn't.

Winning and keeping management buy-in is people's business, which makes it complex. It's like a jigsaw puzzle you must finish. In this case, it consists of fifteen pieces. You can divide the fifteen strategies to win management buy-in for change into three categories. I identified six cultural-related strategies, five strategy-related strategies and four process-related strategies.

All strategies to win management buy-in for change emerged from practice

Some innovators get quite frustrated from all those nos. I did too, at the start of my professional career. And at the same time, I was very persistent, as it was difficult and not acceptable to me that I was stopped by others, while you know you're doing the right thing.

Like you, I just love to do difficult things – otherwise we would not have ended up in innovation, right? I learned innovation by doing, like swimming. Is there any other way?

15 Strategies to Win Management Buy-in to Innovation

CULTURE-RELATED

1 UNDERSTAND YOUR MANAGEMENT'S AGENDA

2 CULTIVATE INNOVATION AMBASSADORS

3 WE-NNOVATE ACROSS SILOS

4 ASSEMBLE A TOP TEAM

5 EXPERIMENT

6 BE A GREAT INNOVATOR

STRATEGY-RELATED

7 SEIZE THE INNOVATION SWEET SPOT

8 ALIGN INNOVATION TO STRATEGY

9 SHOWCASE INNOVATION SUCCESSES

10 FIND INNOVATION PARTNERS

11 BE CUSTOMER-CENTRED

PROCESS-RELATED

12 APPLY PROVEN METHODS

13 PROVE CUSTOMER COMMITMENT

14 DRAFT AN INNOVATION BUSINESS CASE

15 PITCH YOUR STORY

Learning to innovate is like learning to swim

When you want to learn to swim,

you can go to the library and read a book about swimming.

You can visit a swimming pool and watch people swim.

You can interview swimmers in the water at the edge of the pool on what it's like to swim.

You can ask swimmers to demonstrate how they swim.

And you can even put your hand in the water to imagine how it would feel.

But the only way to really learn to swim is to jump into the water.

It's the same with innovation.

All the strategies I am sharing with you I learned by doing, by being a corporate innovator, strategy consultant, innovation facilitator and speaker on design thinking innovation. Let's check them out.

Six Cultural-related Strategies

Innovation doesn't just happen within the confines of a single person, department, or team. It thrives in a corporate culture that fosters creativity, collaboration, and openness to new ideas. Cultural-related strategies focus on transforming the mindset and behaviour of individuals within the organisation, creating an environment where innovation can flourish.

I define a culture for innovation as *"an environment that encourages people to think creatively, which leads to ideas for new products, processes, business models and approaches which are transformed into reality swiftly, creating impact for the organisation."*

By understanding your management's agenda, cultivating innovation ambassadors, breaking down silos, assembling top teams, embracing experimentation, and by being a great innovator, you can lay the foundation for a culture of innovation that inspires and empowers every member of your organisation, including top management.

1. Understand your management's agenda: To effectively pitch innovation ideas to your management team or board, it's crucial to understand their priorities, goals, and concerns. Take the time to align your innovation proposals with their personal goals and the broader objectives of the organisation. Ideally you demonstrate how your innovation initiative address key challenges and opportunities. Using your emotional intelligence you create a personal relationship, understand their agenda, and imagine how innovation can play a role delivering personal value to them.

2. Cultivate innovation ambassadors: You start fostering a culture of innovation within your organisation by identifying and empowering innovation ambassadors at all levels and across all silos. You might form an informal 'innovation gang' or a more formal 'innovation club'. It's a great recipe that works even in the most conservative organisations, as there are people with 'likewise innovative minds'. All these individuals might help you in an informal way to prioritise innovation, help champion new ideas, get innovation team members on board, inspire their peers to say yes, and facilitate communication between frontline innovators and top management.

3. We-nnovate across silos: all medium-sized and big organisations are silo-ed, working somewhat next to each other or even against each other by fighting for priority, people and resources. Breaking down silos within your organisation is essential for innovation by fostering personal relations, collaboration, and cross-functional teamwork. Instead of I-nnovating for myself, my department, or my region, we will be we-nnovating our organisation. It will encourage employees from different departments to share ideas, leverage diverse perspectives, and work together to create great radical new solutions. The Innovation Stories of Bruil, CCI, Huntsman, SEA and NTT DATA highlight the advantages of a we-nnovation approach.

4. Assemble a top team: Innovation is people's business. For a great innovation performance, it's essential to build a team of talented individuals who are passionate about innovation and have the skills and expertise needed to drive change. Empower this team to take ownership of innovation projects and provide them with the resources and support they need to succeed. Gaining trust of senior management that the team will deliver on the innovation challenge is essential to win their buy-in.

5. Experiment: Uncertainty prevails at the start of the innovation process. A lot of people might have outspoken opinions on the project. But nobody knows. That's why experimenting is essential. It creates feedback on both the attractiveness of the new concept and the feasibility: what works and what doesn't. Embracing experimentation in a 'safe zone' in the organisation supports the 'fail fast or scale fast' approach. Learning from market feedback and pivoting to new versions quickly is a way to win trust and buy-in from senior management to continue to fund and support your innovation project. That's completely supported by the Innovation Story on an experimentation safe zone at SAP in Germany.

6. Be a great innovator: As an innovator you are part of the game. Winning management buy-in for innovation means also win-buy for yourself, as you are leading innovation. Your soft skills and your personality make the difference. Venture capitalists use the horse and jockey analogy: do you say yes because of the jockey (the person) or because of the horse (the idea). Winning buy-in is based on trust. It's based on trust of senior management that you are the right jockey to ride the horse. And personality creates trust.

Five Strategy-related Strategies

While a culture of innovation provides the necessary groundwork, strategic alignment ensures that innovation efforts are directed towards the most promising opportunities for growth and success. Innovation is a management instrument. And relating it to how it can deliver strategic goals helps you to get innovation prioritised and improve your innovation performance. By seizing the innovation sweet spot, aligning innovation to strategy, showcasing past successes, finding external partners, and putting customers at the centre of innovation, organisations can ensure that their innovation efforts are focused, strategic, and impactful.

1. Seize the innovation sweet spot: Most of the time "the business of today beats innovation for tomorrow". So, you as an innovator should have the patience to pick the right moment. Why? Because you only have one shot. There are two sweet spots in the lifecycle of an organisation where innovation gets priority. Focusing your innovation efforts on alignment with organisational capabilities and strategic priorities will create priority at the right moment, when senior managers are ready to buy-in. The Innovation Story of Huntsman in Europe will help you find the right moment.

2. Align innovation to strategy: Ensure that your innovation initiatives are closely aligned with the overall strategic direction of the organisation. Clearly articulate how innovation supports key business objectives and contributes to long-term growth and success. A wonderful tool to use is drafting an innovation assignment. Especially moments when a new CEO is onboarding or when a new strategy is presented form great opportunities to win management buy-in for innovation. A great example of how innovation supports a new strategy can be found in the Innovation Story of CCI, a manufacturer of sweets in the Netherlands.

3. Showcase innovation successes: Although it might be some time ago, I am sure that your organisation has had its innovation successes in the past. Highlighting the tangible benefits and outcomes of past innovation projects, helps you to demonstrate the value of investing in future initiatives and to win management buy-in. Use case studies, testimonials, and metrics from your organisations, from other sectors or countries to quantify the positive impact of innovation on revenue growth, customer satisfaction, and other key performance indicators.

4. Find innovation partners: Being connected to other people, firms and institutions who can add complementary benefits is key in accelerating innovation, mitigating risks, and unlocking new opportunities for growth. So, ride the open innovation wave and start collaborating with external partners, such as customers, suppliers, universities, and start-ups, to access new ideas, technologies, and market insights.

5. Be customer-centred: Innovation provides new solutions for relevant customer challenges. Without customers there is no business model. Prioritise understanding customer needs and preferences throughout the innovation process is key for a successful outcome. Conduct user research and involve lead users in co-creation activities to ensure that your innovation efforts are aligned with market demand.

Four process-related strategies

Even with the right cultural mindset and strategic direction, innovation can fail without effective processes and methodologies in place. A lot of organisations do not have a structured new product development process in place. That's why I share four process-related strategies to win management buy-in for changing the focus on streamlining the innovation process, reducing risk, and maximizing the chances of success. Applying proven methodologies, securing customer commitments, developing robust innovation business cases, and crafting compelling innovation stories creates confidence and clarity. These strategies help you to turn innovative ideas into tangible outcomes, driving sustainable growth and competitive advantage.

1. Apply proven methodologies: Adopting established innovation methodologies and techniques, makes a lot of sense, as it will reduce uncertainty. Structured approaches increase efficiency and mitigate risks. Many methodologies emphasise cross-functional collaboration, breaking silos by bringing together diverse perspectives and expertise within the organisation. This fosters creativity and innovation by leveraging the collective intelligence of the team. You get fifty methods and techniques presented later, of which I will recommend ten to help you streamline your innovation process and increase the likelihood of success. The Innovation Story of NTT DATA in Japan will show you methodologies that helped to create buy-in for new solutions at their customers.

2. Prove customer commitment: Demonstrating the market demand for your innovation ideas by securing commitments from potential customers or partners is a very convincing way to win buy-in for innovation. Customers that co-create new solutions validate the viability of your new concepts and reduce the perceived risk for your senior managers to say yes.

3. Draft an innovation business case: History has shown us that a lot of wise people haven't been able to recognise the potential of a great idea. The most essential question your senior managers might ask is, "Why should I fund the development of this new innovation?" Developing a convincing innovation business case, outlining the potential costs, benefits, risks, and return on investment helps your management team make informed decisions. You will get a proven framework of a 9-paged innovation business case and will learn from the Innovation Story of Bruil that built a radical 3D innovation business case in the concrete sector in the Netherlands.

4. Pitch your innovation story: Craft a persuasive and engaging story that communicates the vision, purpose, and impact of your innovation initiative. Make sure your pitch will resonate with your senior managers, addressing their specific concerns, priorities, and personal goals. A great story always resonates. And that's why and when it gets you buy-in for change. It will open the eyes of those who are imprisoned in historical successes, or the business of today, and will get you the support you need to start a new journey: delivering your innovation.

By mastering these fifteen strategies, you will pave your way to becoming an immensely impactful innovator, earning the trust, support, and buy-in of your management team to drive meaningful change and drive organisational success.

I will extensively explain each of the strategies to win management buy-in for change in the following chapters, alternated by great innovation stories from all over the world. Let's dig into Strategy 1. Understand your Management's Agenda, in the next chapter.

Key messages from this chapter:

☞ Winning management buy-in for innovation is a complex jigsaw puzzle.

☞ Mastering fifteen strategies helps you drive meaningful change and innovation.

☞ First, you help your managers to prioritise innovation.

☞ Second, you satisfy your senior managers with a great innovation performance.

☞ Third, you win your managers' buy-in to keep your innovation projects alive and kicking.

Gijs van Wulfen

"Impactful innovators turn nos into yesses."

CULURE-RELATED STRATEGY

1 Understand your Management's Agenda

IMPACTS MOST

10 NOT FITTING MANAGERS' GOALS

IMPACTS ALSO

12 NO PRIORITY TO INNOVATE

13 NO CLEAR DIRECTION TO INNOVATE

You will likely get a no when your innovation efforts don't fit your superiors' agenda. Understanding your senior managers' agenda is key to picking the right moment for innovation. It will help you prioritise innovation and get a clear direction for innovation.

Beware of Planting Bulbs in Unfertile Soil

As a Dutchman, you will believe me when I say that you should have planted tulips last autumn if you wanted to have tulips in spring. Building on this metaphor, as an innovator, you should beware of planting your bulbs in unfertile soil, such as in winter or summer. If you want to have great flowering tulips, you must work the soil first. I learned the hard way that the same applies to innovation. The soil, as you understand already, is your organisation.

Innovation is not a goal as such. As you have read before, it's an instrument to reach all kinds of strategic goals. If you want your management to support innovation, you must understand what's in their scope and what's important for them. The scope in which you innovate can be quite diverse among organisations. The CEO of a family business might have the freedom to look five or ten years ahead. In contrast, the CEO of a company listed on a stock exchange has a much shorter planning horizon, focusing more on delivering results according to quarterly forecasts.

Innovation is not only the scope of an R&D Director or Chief Technology Officer (CTO). Innovation is a way to develop and grow a firm in the long term, so it's relevant for the whole C-suite and their management team. The Chief Executive Officer (CEO), the Chief Commercial Officer (CCO), the Chief Technical Officer (CTO), the Chief Financial Officer (CFO), and the Chief Information Officer (CIO) are all relevant to them. You might even have a dedicated Chief Innovation Officer (CINO) who is primarily responsible for innovation.

Twenty-five years ago, the Chief Innovation Officer role was virtually unheard of. Today, roughly 30 per cent of *Fortune 500* companies have a Chief Innovation Officer. It's interesting to note that Harvard Business Review abbreviates it as CINO. I won't make the joke that it's because the person is overwhelmed by nos all the time – ciNO!

Different Backgrounds Create Different Expectations

Depending on their role, attitude, and background, senior managers and C-suite executives may see innovation quite differently and expect different outcomes.

Assume there's a dedicated innovation director in your management team or a CINO amongst your executives. Their expectations of what innovation is about and what is to be delivered may vary greatly depending on their backgrounds, as you can see.

Six Different Innovation Hats of the Chief Innovation Officer (CINO) [1]

A CINO or innovation director can, based on their background, wear different innovation hats with different definitions and expectations.

The researcher defines innovation "the invention of entirely new things".	The engineer defines innovation "always working to make something a little bit". better".	The investor defines innovation "the way to big growth".	The advocate defines innovation "delivering something new for the customer".	The motivator defines innovation "unlocking the ideas of others".	The organiser defines innovation "a clear process for developing new ideas".

So, get to know your innovation director or CINO first to get a proper impression of his or her background and how they define innovation.

The researcher, the engineer, the investor, the advocate, the motivator, and the organiser all have different perspectives, all valid and true.

Understanding the agenda of your senior managers and CEO is key to bringing innovation onto the corporate agenda. Understanding them depends on the context of your conversations with them and, foremost, on the relationship you can build with them. Once you know what's on their agenda, you can imagine when and how innovation could play a role in helping them attain their targets. You can also decide better when to pitch your call to action, to prioritise innovation or to launch a new concept.

Be Emotionally Intelligent

As an innovator, you benefit from using your emotional intelligence. Emotionally intelligent people are good at thinking about how other people might feel and understand their own feelings. It is:

- An ability to identify and describe what people are feeling.
- An awareness of personal strengths and limitations.
- Self-confidence and self-acceptance.
- The ability to let go of mistakes.
- An ability to accept and embrace change.
- A strong sense of curiosity, particularly about other people.
- Feelings of empathy and concern for others.
- Showing sensitivity to the feelings of other people.
- Accepting responsibility for mistakes.
- The ability to manage emotions in difficult situations.

A large part of emotional intelligence is thinking about and empathising with other people's feelings. Empathy plays a crucial role in building strong relationships with senior managers. It allows you to understand their perspectives, needs, and concerns.

When your internal efforts to prioritise change are failing, it's wise to invest time in understanding your management's agenda. I will provide you with the following four-step approach to do so in a structured way.

1. Identify Key Innovation Decision Makers

First, identify who's involved in the internal decision-making on innovation. In medium and big organisations, several management layers are often involved, and on each level, there are probably more people from different departments, divisions, or business units. Map all the relevant persons involved and identify their roles, which might be a) deciders, b) gatekeepers, or c) influencers.
The decision-making unit on innovation may vary depending on the phase you're in in your innovation process. Strategically prioritising innovation will involve quite a group of formal decision-makers from your management team (and the C-suite) and an official go-to-launch decision for a new concept on the market. Progressing through the (stage-gated) innovation process might be delegated to a specific steering committee or even just one senior manager.

2. Relate to Understand Their Agenda

Focus on your top decision-makers and build a personal relationship with them. Be empathic and curious. Take the initiative and ask for a short getting-to-know-you meeting if you are interested in them. Relate to them with the goal of understanding their personal agendas.

Most organisations have a performance-based compensation or incentive system for senior managers. At the top of the personal agenda of your senior managers is always securing their personal financial bonus at the end of the year. The parameters that might be part of measuring the performance of a CEO are mostly based on the company's strategy and might be:

- Increasing the annual revenue by twenty per cent through innovative product/service expansions and market penetration strategies.
- Achieving a thirty per cent reduction in operational costs by streamlining internal processes and improving efficiency.
- Expanding global market presence by entering three new emerging markets.
- Enhancing customer satisfaction by achieving a seventy or higher Net Promoter Score (NPS).
- Leading industry sustainability efforts by reducing the carbon footprint by fifty per cent.

When it comes to your managers, it would be great if you could identify their personal performance goals, as they will be open to any strategy or initiative that would help them realise these goals.

You might start by showing genuine interest in your senior manager's well-being and celebrating their successes. Meet him or her as often as you can at so-called 'Watercooler Moments' or 'Coffee Machine Moments' for an informal chat. By demonstrating empathy, you can show them that you value their feelings and experiences, which fosters trust, mutual respect, and cooperation. Use your skills of active listening, being kind and non-judgmental. Ask – when the relationship is strong enough – what's on their agenda, and what their goals are for the short and longer term. Ask them also questions about the strategic challenges or issues they are confronting. The better you understand the needs and challenges of your managers, the bigger the chance of convincing them.

3. Imagine How Innovation Can Help Your Management's Goals

Once you know what's on their mind and what their challenges are, imagine how innovation can help to solve them and help attain their goals. When innovation can solve a specific challenge or make a wish of theirs come true, you have their attention.

Here, you will find a list of eight factors and issues that matter to CEOs.

What Matters Most? Eight Priorities for CEOs. [2]

In 'What Matters Most? Eight Priorities for CEOs in 2024', McKinsey & Company reveals eight factors that will take up your CEO's time.

1. Focusing on Gen AI: Which segments of our company can benefit from Gen AI? How to scale the type of usage across departments.
2. Keeping up with technology: While most companies have undergone a digital and AI transformation, many are still not necessarily seeing the expected impact.
3. The energy transition: CEOs will push ahead with bold moves regarding sustainability.
4. Knowing what elevates you: What's our organisation's unique superpower?
5. Appreciating middle management: CEOs will be considering new ways to celebrate and reward middle managers for the work they do and want to continue doing.
6. Geopolitical resilience: CEOs must consider how best to position themselves to be successful amidst current and ongoing upheaval in the global arena.
7. Keep growing (obviously): Our path to growth remains top-of-mind for company leaders.
8. The fluctuating macroeconomy: Regardless of how the economy shifts, CEOs will use scenario planning to get ahead of the curve.

Can innovation solve one of the top five issues in your organisation or your clients?

4. Get Innovation on the Agenda

Depending on your senior managers' goals and your organisation's challenges, you have to package innovation differently to get it on your management's agenda. How? Let's take the eight priorities of CEOs as a starting point and pitch to prioritise innovation accordingly.

1. Focusing on Gen AI: "Let's start an AI Innovation Scaling project." And develop new ways to accelerate the use of AI amongst departments.
2. Keeping up with technology: "Let's start an Innovation Accelerate Impact project." And create new ways to boost the impact of AI and digitalisation on business results.
3. The energy transition: "Let's start an Innovation Carbon Neutrality Booster." And identify new ways to achieve carbon neutrality in five years.
4. Knowing what elevates us: "Let's start an internal innovation project identifying new ways to unleash our organisation's superpower to boost results."
5. Appreciating middle management: "Let's start a middle management Innovation project." And generate new revolutionary ways to celebrate and reward middle managers.
6. Geopolitical resilience: "Let's start a Geopolitical Innovation Programme." And come up with new approaches to de-risk our exposure to worldwide crises.
7. Keep growing: "Let's start an Innovation for Growth Initiative." And identify new revolutionary ways to boost our company's growth in the upcoming five years.
8. The fluctuating macroeconomy: "Let's Start an Ahead-of-the-Curve Innovation Programme." And generate new ways to anticipate and proactively respond to big economic shifts.

Or when you take the first three personal goals of your CEO mentioned above as starting points, you could get innovation on the agenda in the following way:

- ☛ Increase annual revenue: "Let's start a Quick Win Innovation Programme." And identify new product/service expansions with high growth potential.
- ☛ Reduction in operational costs: "Let's start a COSTOVATION project." And identify revolutionary ways of operational process innovation with huge cost-saving potential.
- ☛ Expand Global Market Presence: "Let's Start a Market Innovation Programme." And identify and enter three new emerging markets with great potential.

As you read above, when you want to get innovation on your management's agenda, the regular "Let's develop new products, services, or business models" approach will not work. It's way too general.

As innovation transforms new ideas into reality with impact, you get it on the agenda by tailoring it to solve the issues that matter most to your management team and C-suite and/or help realise their personal performance goals. Understanding their agenda is key.

The good news is that to win management buy-in for change, you will be more successful if you have others on your side helping you prioritise innovation. That's why the next chapter focuses on cultivating innovation ambassadors.

Key Messages from This Chapter:

☞ When you want your management to support innovation, you must understand what's important to them.

☞ Expectations of what innovation is about vary greatly depending on the backgrounds of your managers.

☞ Identify the key innovation decision-makers and relate to them to understand their goals and challenges.

☞ Tailor innovation as a solution for senior managers to help them realise their personal performance goals.

[1] *Harvard Business Review*. https://hbr.org/2019/11/what-kind-of-chief-innovation-officer-does-your-company-need
[2] https://strategyonline.ca/2024/01/09/what-will-be-on-the-minds-of-ceos-in-2024/

Gijs van Wulfen

"Did you
why a Chief
Officer is

ever wonder
Innovation
called
a ciNO...?"

2 Cultivate Innovation Ambassadors

IMPACTS MOST

SHORT-TERM FOCUS

IMPACTS ALSO

CULTURAL NORMS

BUREAUCRACY

Winning management buy-in for change is a tough job. By cultivating innovation ambassadors, you mobilise internal professionals and influencers to help the organisation move beyond their short-term focus to generate new solutions for 'the day after tomorrow'. Informal or formal innovation ambassadors, help you also to change the conservative cultural norms and to solve all the red tape that slows down decision-making and innovation.

Innovation ambassadors help you build bridges

You can foster a culture of innovation within your organisation by identifying and empowering innovation ambassadors at all levels and across all silos. It's a great recipe which I have seen to work in very conservative organisations. Even in traditionalist organisations there are always like-minded people with open minds and a passion to innovate. These individuals might help you in a formal or informal way to create awareness for innovation, prioritise innovation, help champion new ideas, get innovation team members on board, inspire their peers to say yes, and facilitate communication between innovators and top management.

Innovation ambassadors help to build bridges to boost innovation. It can be horizontal between diverse departments, business units or divisions of an organisation. And they can build bridges vertically helping frontline innovators to get buy-in for innovation at senior management.

Of course, you start reaching out to professionals from both 'the business side' of your organisation and the 'technological side'. You invite people from marketing and sales, and from research & development, information technology and production departments.

Including innovation ambassadors from other departments like financial administration, quality control, purchasing, supply chain, human resources, and legal helps you to accelerate innovation, asking their help to solve all the red tape that slows down decision-making and innovation.

Examples of innovation ambassadors

As example of an innovation ambassador programme, I included the initiative of SNAM, a big Italian energy infrastructure company, for their attempt to create a culture for innovation. Their so-called 'Snaminnova programme' is based on three fundamental pillars: external innovation, to enhance the best innovative ideas on the market; internal innovation, to enhance the company's knowledge and experience; and the culture of innovation, to develop and spread culture and innovative thinking within the organisation. The innovation ambassador programme is part of this last pillar.

SNAM's Seventy innovation ambassadors [1]

SNAM is an energy infrastructure company founded in 1941 in Italy, historically active in the transport, storage and regasification of natural gas and today also involved in activities related to energy transition, sustainable mobility, hydrogen, biomethane and energy efficiency. It's listed on the Italian stock market. It has 3,800 employees and a revenue of 4.29 billion euros in 2023.

The 3 pillars of innovation at SNAM

SNAM launched a programme called 'Snaminnova' with the aim of accelerating the innovation process and the exchange of internal and external knowledge. The Snaminnova programme is based on three fundamental pillars: external innovation, to enhance the best innovative ideas on the market; internal innovation, to enhance the company's knowledge and experience; and the culture of innovation, to develop and spread culture and innovative thinking within the organisation.

The innovation ambassador's programme

This last pillar includes the **innovation ambassadors**, introduced into SNAM about three years ago and which, from the initial fifty, have now grown into a group of around seventy. Initially, people were recruited through a free application form on the company's intranet, where the role was described as an opportunity to live an experience of innovation, without further detailed specifications. This allowed SNAM to gather the interest of motivated and passionate resources, who were then selected for the role from a pool of candidates.

Two roles of innovation ambassadors

Firstly, an innovation ambassador is responsible for developing and spreading culture and innovative thinking within the organisation, with the fundamental support of the Human Resources Function for the definition of an appropriate growth path. In addition to this, the innovation ambassadors are responsible for intercepting the innovation needs coming from their business unit and have a leading role in the development of internal entrepreneurship initiatives and in the interaction with the external ecosystem. Specifically with regard to internal innovation, innovation ambassadors play a central role in supporting colleagues who propose innovation ideas. They offer tools and support in defining the reference context, the idea itself, the value proposition, and the business model. The colleagues are then supported until the moment of a real pitch in front of an evaluation committee represented by the SNAM leadership team.

In the case of external innovation, however, the innovation ambassadors act as a bridge between the needs of the business units and the innovative solutions on the market. In this context, innovation ambassadors support the construction of business cases and experimental phases, also acting as beta testers for digital solutions. Finally, with reference to both the external and internal ecosystems, innovation ambassadors build and maintain relationships through participation in events and networking activities.

Skills for an innovation ambassador

To train their skills, innovation ambassadors participate in a rich annual training programme that is divided into two directions. The first concerns inspiration and consists of opportunities to share stories of innovation, entrepreneurship and experiences that generate cultural contamination. The second direction concerns more technical training, with the development of skills, tools, approaches and methodologies typical of open innovation.

Soon, the objectives that SNAM sets for the development of this role include the expansion of the community within the company, the consolidation of the role at an organizational level and the extension of networking and discussion opportunities with the open innovation ecosystem.

It's a great opportunity to expand the innovation ambassador programme also beyond your own organisation, reaching out to external partners. I will discuss the advantages of creating an open innovation ecosystem later in this book in Strategy 10: find innovation partners.

How to cultivate innovation ambassadors

When innovation is not embraced by everyone yet, it's a great strategy to build an informal 'innovation gang' first, before suggesting to your senior management to start a more formal 'innovation ambassador programme'. You only start the latter when you are hundred per cent sure that it will get adequate support at top level.

I have seven tips for you how to cultivate innovation ambassadors and create an official innovation ambassador's platform. Check them out here:

1. **Start informal.** First and only to contact people internally who you know and trust. Invite them for informal innovation gatherings where you share the why and your specific goals to foster a culture for innovation. Grow the informal movement by a member-gets-member approach, which will expand it across the organisation. Be aware that people will approach you too to be part of this new network and embrace them all. Do not make it an 'exclusive club' but an inclusive movement for everyone who wants to innovate.
2. **Define innovation.** We all know the principle of innovation, but how exactly do we define it? So, make immediately clear what innovation stands for. This is essential to move the innovation ambassadors in a common direction.
3. **Work out the role.** Define also the concrete role of the innovation ambassadors and discuss the expectations about their activities. My tip is to create a role of innovation ambassadors as 'facilitators of innovation'. This means they are building bridges between people and departments to contribute to winning buy-in for change and promoting innovation.
4. **Scale-up the initiative.** Once, with the help of the 'informal innovation movement', you stand a fair chance to prioritise innovation at senior level, you might bring the initiative 'above ground' and scale-up to a formal innovation ambassador platform.
5. **Get everyone in.** Engage an active sponsor within the C-suite as primary sponsor. And enrol a fair distribution according to professions and departments mixing both employees and high-ranked managers. Diversity is key to a culture of innovation.
6. **Train skills.** Inspire and train the mindsets and soft skills of the innovation ambassadors as innovation facilitators. And provide them with proven simple techniques and methods to help others to start innovation and deliver results accordingly.
7. **Reward ambassadors.** Make your programme rewarding for innovation ambassadors. An innovation ambassador invests time and undertakes actions supporting the creation of a culture for innovation. Make the programme, and the meetings engaging and rewarding for them. You might get it included, in collaboration with the human resource department, as part of their performance bonus.
8. **Share learnings.** Facilitate sharing of all new insights, learnings and results achieved both within your meetings as well as in the organisation.

Seven tips to start an 'Innovation Ambassadors Programme'.

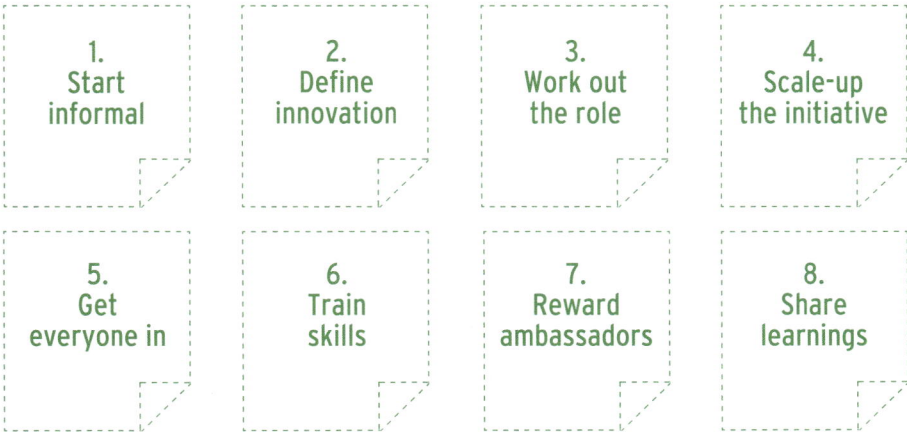

1. Start informal	2. Define innovation	3. Work out the role	4. Scale-up the initiative
5. Get everyone in	6. Train skills	7. Reward ambassadors	8. Share learnings

So by cultivating innovation ambassadors, you mobilise internal professionals and influencers to help your organisation move beyond the short-term focus to generate new solutions for 'the day after tomorrow'. It's also a great support for the strategy in the next chapter to We-nnovate across departments.

Key Messages from This Chapter:

☞ Innovation ambassadors help build bridges.

☞ Create a role of innovation ambassadors as 'facilitators of innovation'.

☞ Start in an informal way to scale-up later.

☞ Include professionals from all departments.

☞ Expand the innovation ambassador programme beyond your own organisation in a later stage.

[1] https://www.economyup.it/innovazione/snam-cosi-gli-innovation-ambassador-promuovono-linnovazione-interna-ed-esterna/

Gijs van Wulfen

"The speed organisation is the slowest

of your determined by ones."

3 We-nnovate across Silos

IMPACTS MOST

6 ORGANISA-TIONAL SILOS

IMPACTS ALSO

2 LACK OF DIVERSITY

12 NO PRIORITY TO INNOVATE

Organisational silos are hindering change and innovation. By we-nnovating across silos you engage and connect all relevant professionals, uniting their goals, interests, and approaches. By including people from the entire organisation, you solve the lack of diversity. And because you stand stronger together, you are more likely to win management buy-in for change.

You can't innovate alone: so we-nnovate

I learned a wise lesson: 'You can invent on your own, but you can't innovate alone'.

How many colleagues, managers, and partners you need in your (client's) organisation to get your vision transformed into a new product, service, experience, process, or business model and get it launched?

You need R&D engineers, production managers, IT staff, financial controllers, marketers, service people, and salespeople to develop your concept, produce it, get it launched, and service it.

Ideas are like children. That's why we-nnovation works!

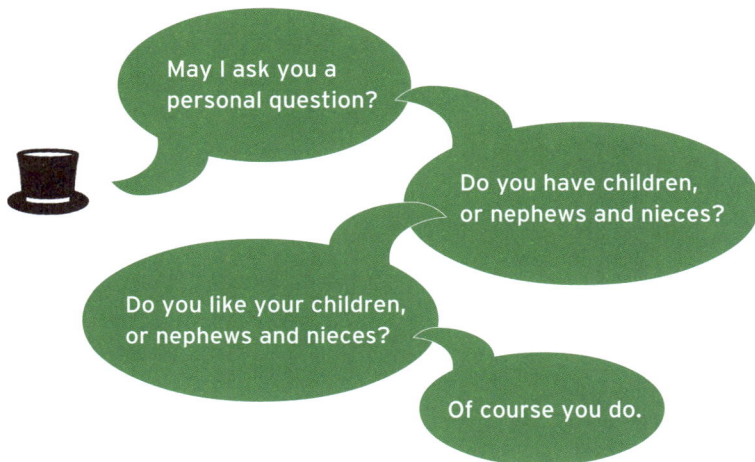

May I ask you a personal question?

Do you have children, or nephews and nieces?

Do you like your children, or nephews and nieces?

Of course you do.

Do you like the children of the neighbours?

Do you have neighbours with children, or neighbours of neighbours with children?

Of course you do, most of the time.

Do you love the children of the neighbours?

Now... That's different. Know that the only difference between your child and the child of your neighbours is that your child is yours, and the child of the neighbours is not ... probably!

IT'S THE SAME WITH IDEAS. Ideas are like children.
Does your partner, or, in my case, ex-partner, also love your children?
Of course. That's no coincidence. You love your children because they have your DNA, you made them together and you care for them together.

People reject your idea because for them it's the neighbours' child, not theirs.

The best way to get ideas accepted is to co-create or we-nnovate, as I like to call it. It means you're creating innovative ideas together and stretching your comfort zones together, instead of ending up frustrated and feeling rejected.

That's why you should ideate together – you brainstorm new ideas with everyone who will be involved in the realisation process of your idea. Because as a parent, you will stretch your comfort zone endlessly to take care of your own child!

Ideas are like children. You only really love ideas when your DNA is in them. So that's why the only way to get real buy-in for change is to co-create together in the innovation process. That's when you apply 'we-nnovation' instead of 'i-nnovation'.

Now, while we-nnovating, don't make the mistake of surrounding yourself with only the so-called innovators. Your organisation is like a herd. The herd goes as fast as the slowest animal. If the non-innovators lean back, nothing moves. The way to get people to be more innovative is to respect them, to understand them, to connect with them, and to let them experience that innovation is necessary. They will only change their attitudes if they get new insights themselves. So create a situation where they discover what is happening in the world: how markets, customers, competitors, and technologies are changing. Talking to customers with varying needs, finding new competitors, and exploring new technologies will open them up. That's how you create momentum for 'we-nnovation'.

Six best practices that make diversity work

The Boston Consulting Group (BCG) concludes that firms that really make diversity work, those that maximise the variety of ideas and then select the best for scaling-up, are significantly more likely to outperform their peers [1]. They implement the following six best practices, which I would like to share with you:

1. **Mix and match diverse teams.** Create teams that go beyond compositional diversity and show genuine functional diversity by having staffing mechanisms that consider metrics of such diversity. GetYourGuide, a global travel and tourism player, ensured that the foreign-born talent it recruited was spread through the organisation, avoiding monocultural silos of any nationality or origin, which can often work effectively but lose their creative edge.

2. **Circulate innovators globally.** Set up internal migration networks to attract daring, unconventional problem solvers from a variety of geographic locations. BCG's think tank, the BCG Henderson Institute, for example, offers secondments for BCG employees to physically relocate to one of its innovation hubs and explore a new research topic. Programmes like this should be framed as an innovation rotation – a valuable career step towards leadership that is supported by top management.

3. **Break organisational boundaries.** Set up circular externship programmes with smaller, faster growing organisations. Earlier this year, BCG encouraged

employees to join a rapidly growing pharmaceutical company producing COVID-19 vaccines. BCG regularly offers its employees growth opportunities like this, because it believes in the innovative exchange that results from such deployments.

4. **Foster divergence.** Shape a culture that respects the individual and values new ideas irrespective of place in hierarchy, for example by having regular exchange forums to test ideas under pressure in a trusted environment. Stripe, a global financial services firm, forms internal interest groups based on origin. These groups have a dual purpose; first, they provide a second 'home' to foreign talent at Stripe, which helps to build the employer brand, and second, they play an active role in customising products and go-to-market strategy for global markets.

5. **Remain mission-first.** Train innovation managers to create alignment in multicultural, multi-functional teams and to guide their teams towards maximal outcomes. Tech companies often pride themselves in creating a culture that celebrates the focus and goal-mindedness of 'missionaries' in service of their purpose, often a customer need, over 'mercenaries'; managers managing perception first, outcomes second.

6. **Guide via a pragmatic decision-making process.** Guide diverse innovation teams towards maximised outcomes or fast failure, by subjecting them to a lean decision process that ensures that the best projects survive. While nearly all companies have such staggered funding logic processes, they often fail to produce desired outcomes because teams are either not empowered or not incentivised to recommend a course correction or a project shutdown.

An effective process to foster a we-nnovation culture

The FORTH innovation methodology, founded by me, is a structured approach to innovation that focuses on finding, filtering, fast-tracking, and fostering innovative ideas for successful implementation. It combines design thinking and business thinking in a structured way. Due to the length and intensity of the programme, it creates a long lasting impact, fostering a culture for we-nnovation, as I will explain below.

FORTH is used when organisations want to create a culture for innovation across all silos and systematically want to innovate by identifying promising ideas, refining them, and swiftly bringing them to market. It works by first drafting an innovation assignment and assemble a top team. It consists of ten professionals across all silos in the core-team. And of five senior managers actively participating in the most important workshops as an extended team (Full Steam Ahead). Then you gather new insights and needs of clients through exploration (Observe & Learn). It's followed by generating new ideas and concepts (Raise ideas). Then you filter and select the most promising ones. And you fast-track their development through testing (Test Ideas). Finally, you foster their implementation and scale concepts by drafting new business cases at the end of the innovation journey (Homecoming).

The result of the FORTH innovation method is five new business cases for successful innovations, while sparking a culture for innovation. The three main take-aways are: a structured approach to start innovation, a focus on winning management buy-in for change, and a systematic way to foster a culture of innovation. The process takes around five months from the kick-off onwards, and it has proven to double the innovation effectiveness of stage-gate processes.

The FORTH innovation method

Why does this method help to win management buy-in for change? Let me explain three important mechanisms:

1. When senior managers create an innovation assignment, together they create a common view on innovation and the expected outcomes.
2. When five senior managers are not in a steering committee but are participating actively in the process for at least seven times, they are engaged as their DNA is also generated in the new concepts.
3. When each of the five senior managers adopts one of the five chosen concepts to develop into a new business case as a so-called godfather or godmother, they all know each new business case, and the customer's commitment to it, down to the last detail.

In the previous chapter, I presented you an innovation ambassador platform, an (in) formal structure to create innovation ambassadors who facilitate innovation and build bridges across organisational silos. The we-nnovation process I presented in this chapter is perfectly complementary, creating an approach by which professionals create new innovations together, supported by their senior managers.

After the Innovation Story of SEA on innovating across silos, I will share my views on how to create a top innovation team to initiate innovation through the FORTH process or any other proven innovation methodology.

Key Messages from This Chapter:

☞ You can invent on your own, but you can't innovate alone.

☞ Including people from across the organisation solves the lack of diversity.

☞ You only really love ideas when your DNA is in them.

☞ Get senior managers to participate actively in innovation, instead of only being part of a steering committee.

[1] BCG. https://www.bcg.com/publications/2022/innovation-without-borders-era-with-global-talent

Gijs van Wulfen

"You can invent alone, but you can only innovate together."

INNOVATING ACROSS SILOS AT SEA AREOPORTI MILANO

By Maria Vittoria Colucci

You know from experience that working on cultural change in organisations is complicated. You often get bogged down in the quicksand of the vague and undefined.

This is why, when SEA Areoporti Milano (SEA) asked me to help them to work on diversity & inclusion, I suggested using a proven methodology, FORTH, to make sure that the outcomes were concrete and measurable. And I knew that within the innovation process itself, we would already be able to experiment and put into practice new diversity and inclusion logics that would benefit the subsequent implementation process.

SEA had already worked on the issue of inclusion through working groups that had produced studies and project hypotheses that had not been followed up on. Our goal now was to put feasible, concrete new solutions in place that would have strong top-down sponsorship. And have real impact.

SEA HANDLES 35 MILLION PASSENGERS A YEAR
SEA operates two airports and three terminals in Lombardy, a highly developed economic region in northern Italy. It is in the top 10 European airports for passenger numbers and top 5 for cargo traffic, handling 35.5 million passengers per year.

SEA has been operating for 75 years, and is a company where the people, around 2.300 as of 2023, have a strong sense of belonging, not only because of the history and business in which it operates, but also because they feel they have an impact on the economy and the surrounding area.

Prior to the pandemic, SEA was implementing a series of projects aimed at leveraging emerging technologies to be more customer-focused, responsive to customer needs, and offering an excellent customer experience. Hence the technological innovation and consolidation of operational excellence in all phases of operations.

With the pandemic, passenger numbers had plummeted in 2020. Therefore, a process of reorganisation and rethinking the business model began, reinforcing the commitment to sustainability and connection with the territory.

Increasing well-being by overcoming prejudices and stereotypes.

An important issue in the evolution of the business model of SEA concerns the need to best represent the values of sustainability, understood in multiple meanings: economic sustainability, environmental sustainability, referring to people and their quality of life, inside and outside the organisation.

Airport passengers par excellence represent humankind in all its meanings, and the task of an airport is to develop a welcoming and inclusive culture, both internally and externally.

The why of SEA at that time was very strong and well-defined, in the words of the CEO:

"The pandemic has taken so much from us, changed the context and forms of work and brought out a common feeling, a new solidarity with colleagues and everyone we meet at airports and the need to work for common goals."

The four sponsors: President Michaela Castelli, CEO Armando Brunini, CFRO Patrizia Savi, and COO Alessandro Fidato wanted to focus on three areas of diversity: gender diversity, age, and sexual orientation. Their goal was to achieve something concrete, impactful not only in the short term but also in the medium term. The criteria by which the feasibility analyses resulting from the innovation process would be evaluated included:

1. Measurable indicators over time, and the definition of the process for verifying and sharing results.
2. A first implementation within a year.
3. Simplicity of implementation.

The strong sponsorship from the top was the key factor that made the innovation possible.

THE METHOD

We used FORTH, a proven innovation methodology combining business thinking and Design Thinking in a structured process with divergent and convergent phases.

The SEA innovation team was composed of two groups: the first, core team, works more intensively on the process and is usually composed of eight to ten people. The second team, the extended team, is composed of senior managers with decision-making power, usually four to five people who participate only at certain times to share the directions of innovation, give their creative input, and decide on the best concepts.

In our case, we wanted to represent the diversity present in the company already in the core team to facilitate the innovation process and the grounding of the resulting solutions. That is why the core team was extremely large, 27 people, and the extended team consisted of seven people.

In an airport, professions coexist that differ considerably in terms of professional culture, approach, and mindset. In the case of SEA, the main terminals Linate and Malpensa are very different. In addition to being in Milan and Varese, there was also an additional element of cultural differentiation related to the two locations. For this reason, it was essential to have people from the two locations, from different professions and hierarchical levels, working together in the innovation team. We had to break down functional and hierarchical silos to give everyone a voice. The danger was that, once the areas of innovation were identified, people would resist implementation, considering the topic unimportant or the usual fad pulled out by a group of experts and managers far removed from them.

So the project manager issued a company-wide call for action, asking people to participate in our FORTH project that would innovate diversity & inclusion practices and policies.

The response was very encouraging: around hundred people with a wide variety of roles and professions applied.

Thus, the team was formed with participants from operational and staff areas in the three terminals: Linate, Malpensa 1 and Malpensa 2. And it was composed of different levels ranging from shift workers, white collars, business professionals, people managers, operational managers and executives, from all over SEA as you can see.

SEA INNOVATION TEAM COMPOSITION

The team was composed of different levels ranging from shift workers, white collars, business professionals, people managers, operational managers and executives, from all over SEA:

LINATE	13
Charges Management	1
Corporate Affairs & Compl. Leg. Cseling	1
Credit Management	1
Internal Communication	1
Legal Affairs	1
Legal Affairs – Operations	1
Non-Aviation Marketing Development	1
People Engag., Emp. Brand. & Comp. Mngmt	1
Retail – Shops	1
Security Compliance	1
Security Operations Linate	2
Welfare	1

MALPENSA	14
Airport Op.rs & PA Leasing Management	1
Aviation Marketing, Neg & TR	1
Destination Management	1
Fire Prev. & Work Safety Emerg. Mgmnt	1
HR Mngmt & Collaboration Applications	1
Operational Planning	1
Premium Services	1
PRM Assistance MXP	1
Procurement Legal Account	1
Security Compliance	1
Security Operations Malpensa	4
TOTAL	27

For many workers, it was the first time they had worked side by side with the HR director, or with their senior managers, side by side. Just as it was the first time managers and management control professionals had brainstormed with operational planning or security people.

In the first few workshops, some people did not know whether to call managers whom they had seen only at extended company meetings or conventions 'tu' or 'lei'; someone even asked me: "How did I do?".

Everyone was very excited and involved to be in the group that would innovate diversity & inclusion in their company. Therefore, at first, we had people work in more homogeneous groups by level and then gradually mixed people more in the innovation exercises.

This allowed from the very beginning to have input that came from the work experience of the whole company. In the kick-off for example, we were asked to include among the areas of diversity covered, that of different ability which was not in the areas of focus.

The idea generation workshop was a super high energy event where the groups were now amalgamated, and people felt free to share their new ideas.

The project was an opportunity to learn about the daily work routine and professional culture of completely different areas. The moments when people recounted specific diversity-related episodes, shared ideas generated, a lot of insights, for example of what was going on in the operational areas, and desire to further deepen the knowledge of how they work. Applying three brainstorming techniques on an in-person digital whiteboard, created an amazing number of 2.233 ideas, which were transformed into 43 concepts. Of these, we selected twenty concepts to be tested with internal customers. Thirteen concepts were carried forward after testing, and seven new concepts were worked out into feasibility studies.

As customers were internal people, additional organisational areas were involved in the customer friction detection in Observe & Learn, and test phases. More than 600 people belonging to 43 organisational units participated in this innovation project in interviews, surveys, and focus groups to detect customer frictions and evaluate concepts.

SEVEN INNOVATION PROJECTS APPROVED AND THREE STARTED

The project concluded with the presentation of seven innovative concepts developed and accompanied by as many feasibility studies. They were presented, in the presence of the entire team, to the four sponsors: the president, CEO, CFRO, and COO who gave their assessment and prioritised them for implementation. The sponsors captured the enormous energy, huge enthusiasm, and pride of the people who participated in the project who all became internal sponsors in their areas for implementation.

Part of the team that had developed the solutions became part of the implementation team along with new colleagues whose skills were needed for implementation. Of these projects, three were launched in 2022 and resulted in initiatives that continue to be present in SEA and are even chronicled on their corporate website.

This successful social innovation project has put inclusion on the agenda of many people managers at SEA, creating a long-lasting effect, embedding inclusion in the SEA culture.

FIVE TIPS WHEN INNOVATING ACROSS SILOS

When you want to break innovation barriers in your organisation, especially to win buy-in for innovating across silos, I'd like to share five tips:

1. Involve those departments or units that normally are isolated, have few organisational relationships or have difficulty collaborating with each other.

2. Bringing together different professional cultures with distinctive viewpoints of innovation yields great results, provided you can to create a team spirit of tolerance and psychological safety.

3. Involve all managerial, professional and operational roles to understand potential implementation barriers for new innovative solutions to ensure fluidity of implementation at all levels.

4. Create involvement and strong internal sponsorship at all levels will greatly increase the likelihood of your innovation success.

5. Applying a proven method creates a common language and a common mindset for innovation that changes the way people work within their areas.

Assemble a Top Team

IMPACTS MOST

2 LACK OF DIVERSITY

- -

IMPACTS ALSO

6 ORGANISA-TIONAL SILOS

15 NO CLEAR INNOVATION ROI

In stories of great inventions, like the Melitta case I will share in Strategy 11, we celebrate lone inventors. However, most discoveries these days are made by teams, not lone inventors. Assembling a top innovation team is a must and great strategy to win management buy-in for change. It will build trust from senior managers, as it deals with the lack of diversity and unites innovators across the organisation. Because a top team will be result-oriented, they will focus on delivering a clear innovation return on investment (ROI) too.

I share four perspectives with you: ten traits of effective innovation teams from a business perspective, two important team aspects from a cultural perspective, nine personality types from a role perspective and five success criteria from personal experience over the past twenty years, for a project leader of innovation teams.

Ten key traits of effective innovation teams

Because innovation is a team sport, your innovation projects must be staffed with the right combination of professionals to win management buy-in for change and deliver great outcomes accordingly.

In their innovation research and experiments McKinsey identified ten traits that distinguish the most successful innovators. Many of these capabilities are well-recognised. Your total innovation team performance will benefit from assessing potential individual team members, as the total team needs a base level of competence in all four categories.

- -

Ten Key Traits of Effective Innovation Teams [1]

- -

Vision	**Learning**
1. Uncovering	7. Absorbing
2. Generating	
3. Selling	

- -

Collaboration	**Execution**
4. Motivating	8. Deciding
5. Networking	9. Pioneering
6. Orchestrating	10. Tabulating

- -

Vision. The first group of traits highlights the ability to identify opportunities and inspire others to pursue them. The need to uncover things is an intrinsic curiosity to see the possibility in each context and distil the most valuable insights. Generating is the ability to develop meaningful value propositions that solve significant customer problems. The third trait in this category, selling, is defined as the ability to explain the nuances of what creates the value for a new proposition and carefully tailoring it to the target audience.

Collaboration. Those strong at motivating tend to be charismatic leaders adept at spurring on action by creating a work environment that acceptss failure. Networking is the essential skill in maintaining connections amongst all the stakeholders in a project. Orchestrating refers to the ability to supply projects with the needed resources and to monitor the team's activities to ensure these resources are effectively deployed.

Learning. Absorbing, as McKinsey calls it, is a quality manifested in a deep curiosity in anything that could help their venture succeed and a willingness to explore leads as they arise.

Execution. Deciding encompasses strong critical-thinking skills that enable people to draw conclusions from imperfect information. Pioneering skills enable individuals to break down ideas into an achievable sequence of activities. Tabulating, the last of the ten traits, means the ability to apply financial modelling to size an opportunity and then use scenario planning to de-risk a given project.

To maximise innovation performance, companies should look to balance all the traits evenly in the composition of their innovation teams.

Innovation team culture: cognitively diverse and psychologically safe

It's common knowledge, also in innovation, that the more diverse teams are in terms of age, ethnicity, and gender, the more creative and productive they are likely to be.

Surprisingly however, in their study, Alison Reynolds and David Lewis (HBR) found no correlation between this type of diversity and performance. Instead, they started focusing on cognitive diversity. They define it as: "Differences in perspective or information processing styles. It is not predicted by factors such as gender, ethnicity, or age. Instead, it's all about how individuals think about and engage with new, uncertain, and complex situations". [2] And in additional experiments Reynolds and Lewis discovered that a high degree of cognitive diversity generates accelerated learning and performance in the face of new, uncertain, and complex situations.

Groups that performed well, treated mistakes with curiosity and shared responsibility for the outcomes. As a result, people could express themselves, their thoughts and ideas without fear of social retribution. The team environment they created through their interaction was one of psychological safety: the belief that you won't be punished or humiliated for sharing your ideas, questions, concerns, or mistakes.

The most dominant behaviours and emotions in psychological safe and cognitively diverse groups are:

1. Curiosity
2. Encouragement
3. Experimental
4. Forcefulness
5. Inquisitiveness
6. Nurturing.

So in the team culture, be sure to stimulate and reward these six behaviours to create a top-performing innovation team.

A great team is a mix of personalities

The Mayo Clinic is a best-practice organisation in healthcare innovation located in the USA. When composing innovation teams, they prefer a specific combination of personalities. Of course, you can use the well-known assessment tools like MBTI, Belbin or Four Sight to help to compose a great team. But I love the nine personalities they characterised for an innovation top team. Why? Because these personality types really help you imagine the ideal team. I bet when you read them, people from your own organisation immediately come to mind.

Nine personality types for an innovation top team [3]

The Mayo Clinic strives to include nine specific personality types when composing innovation teams:

The Visionary: The force behind creating the world as it could be – and should be.

The Generator: The generator of the idea that gets an innovation rolling.

The Iterator: An idea-engineer who takes the original idea and turns it into an innovation.

The Customer Anthropologist: The keen observer of what customers truly hunger for.

The Tech Guru: The harnesser of technology to turn the innovation into reality.

The Producer: The champion of flow. The master of moving ideas along.

The Communicator: The one who amplifies and clarifies the idea in the minds of others outside the team.

The Roadblock Remover: Knocks down organisational, political, and financial roadblocks, either with a hammer, or with velvet gloves.

The Futurecaster: The forecaster and modeler of the economic and social value of the future of innovation.

Does your innovation team resemble this combination of personalities?

Five traits of amazing innovation project leaders

For the past twenty years, I facilitated over fifty innovation projects. In a facilitating role, I was always closely connected to the project leader. It's like yin and yang. I led the process, and the internal project leader led the content. Below I'll be sharing the five traits that, in my experience, make an innovation project leader invincible.

1. *Be courageous.* If you accept the job as innovation project leader, you are a hero. Because you accept a huge challenge with only two 'weapons' on hand: a process or methodology, and a team. Accept only challenges worth fighting for, for which you personally are super motivated. And you must stick out your neck, until the (happy) end.
2. *Be strict.* As project leader you must be strict and stay the course. Strict to your senior managers who want to cut time, or budget, or team size or even all three. And strict to your team members, which, having other work too, will try to cut corners, being busy with other things.
3. *Be kind.* When you're strict on 'the hard things', a great project leader is soft on the soft things. When you're kind, all team members (in the end) love to work for you and will deliver.
4. *Be persistent.* Everyone will try to stop you, for whatever reason. And it's your mission to transform nos into yesses. Continuously.
5. *Protect your team.* You are innovating in a conservative organisation, with politics going on 24/7. Others want your status, your budget, your people and your success. Also, your team members will be observed closely, while they're contributing to a major project. Especially when they're not doing well, when they're underperforming or when they're failing, protect them and take responsibility. You will create their eternal loyalty.

The most essential trait of not only the project leader but for everyone in the team, is their passion: everyone has to be thrilled to be part of this particular innovation project, and personally committed to the innovation journey to come.

Composing a top innovation team is essential in winning management buy-in for change, because senior managers place their trust in people. In the next chapter I will be sharing another strategy to de-risk innovation for senior managers: experimenting.

Key messages from this chapter:

☞ A top innovation team masters vision, collaboration, learning and execution.

☞ A top team's culture should be cognitively diverse and psychologically safe.

☞ A top team is composed of nine different personality types.

☞ A project leader should be courageous, strict, kind, and persistent.

☞ By protecting the team, the project leader creates psychological safety.

[1] McKinsey, 'Fielding High-Performance innovation teams', Jan 17, 2019, https://www.mckinsey.com/capabilities/strategy-and-corporate-finance/our-insights/fielding-high-performing-innovation-teams#/
[2] HBR, Alison Reynolds and David Lewis, 'Teams Solve Problems Faster When They're More Cognitively Diverse.' https://hbr.org/2017/03/teams-solve-problems-faster-when-theyre-more-cognitively-diverse
[3] 'Innovation: Putting Ideas into Action 2009 (Best Practices Report)', APQC, Houston, USA.

Robert Kennedy

"Some men see
are, and say
things that
and say

things as they why. I dream of never were, why not?"

5 Experiment

IMPACTS MOST

5 BUREAUCRACY

IMPACTS ALSO

3 FEAR OF FAILURE

11 NO MARKET FOCUS

In big organisations there are all kinds of rules and procedures to protect the current business, which consequently hinder new innovative concepts to accelerate. Experimenting helps you to manoeuvre around these obstacles, as experiments de-risk innovation. Furthermore, presenting outcomes of real-life experiments instead of assumptions, helps you to reduce the fear of failure. Testing concepts and involving real customers are great ways to bring in a market focus in your innovation project, creating more buy-in for change, when customers love the outcomes.

Successful innovations need a pivot

Innovation teams have found that controlled experiments work better than betting on theoretical predictions of success and big-bang releases [1]. A rule of thumb is that two-thirds of successful innovations must significantly change their original plans to achieve their desired objectives. The late innovation expert Clayton Christensen believed this figure was even higher: 93 per cent. Whatever the exact number is, it is higher than most innovation management systems are designed to handle. Now I do not label an unsuccessful test as a failure. It's all about learning, as FAIL is an acronym for a 'first attempt in learning', coined by A.P.J. Abdul Kalam.

By conducting experiments, you can continuously iterate and refine your innovations based on real-time feedback. This iterative approach promotes a culture of continuous improvement, which can be valuable in driving long-term organisational change.

Experimenting mitigates risks and fosters buy-in for radical change

The earlier you experiment with your new solution in practice, the better. Implementing live experiments in a conservative organisation with many bureaucrats can be a bold move, but next to being able to iterate, it comes with three other advantages:

1. *Concrete evidence.* Live experiments provide tangible, real-world evidence of the effectiveness of your new ideas. This concrete data can be more convincing than theoretical arguments, especially in conservative environments where change is approached with caution.

2. *Engagement and buy-in.* Involving stakeholders in live experiments fosters a sense of ownership and engagement. When your senior managers see the impact firsthand, they're more likely to buy into the innovation and support its implementation.

3. *Risk mitigation.* Live experiments allow for testing new ideas on a smaller scale, minimising the risk associated with large-scale implementation. It allows to assess potential risks and benefits before fully committing.

Leading innovators and agile innovation teams have made testing, learning, and adapting a bedrock of their business processes. They set clear objectives and metrics for measuring progress. They bring together experts on various stakeholders to understand their needs and antipathies. They design practical economical experiments. They are transparent about assumptions, uncertainties, and potential dealkillers. They attack the riskiest hypotheses first rather than last. This avoids wasting money on developing easy things for a long time, only to run out of resources and fail near the end.

Create a Minimum Loveable Product (MLP)
When experimenting, innovators like to work with a so-called Minimum Viable Product (MVP), which originated from the Lean Startup movement. But customers, both in consumer markets as well as business markets, are spoiled these days. They have zero tolerance for a frustrating experience, or a product that doesn't work. That's why it would be great when you could exceed expectations from the first interaction with your potential customers, with a so-called Minimum Lovable Product: an MLP instead of an MVP. A Minimum Loveable Product is a term first popularised by Adam Berry, a successful entrepreneur [2]. You create an MLP by asking yourself what is the minimum set of features you need to include to make your users fall in love with your product. And develop and present it to them in that way.

Five types of innovation experiments for attractiveness and feasibility

When you test concepts or MLP's with your customers, there are mostly two crucial questions: 1) Does it work? 2) Do they like it? That's why I'd like to share with you five practical types of experiments through which you can test both the attractiveness and feasibility of a Minimum Loveable Product:

1. *A/B testing.* Create two versions of your MLP, each emphasising different features or business models of the new concept. Launch both versions simultaneously to separate segments of your target audience and measure which version attracts more interest and engagement. This test not only checks the attractiveness, but also helps to assess feasibility by understanding which features of the two resonate most with users.

2. *A limited release.* Launch a limited release of your MLP to a select group of lead users, early adopters or beta testers. This allows you to gather feedback on both the attractiveness and feasibility of the new concept in a real-life setting. Monitor user interactions, gather feedback, and iterate based on insights gained during this experiment.

3. *A pilot programme with innovation partners.* Partner up with a select group of innovation partners or customers to pilot your MLP in a controlled environment. This enables you to test the feasibility of implementation within existing systems or workflows, while also checking the attractiveness of the new concept.

4. *A crowdfunding campaign.* Launch a crowdfunding campaign to introduce your MLP to a wider audience and validate the market demand. By setting specific funding goals and offering early access or exclusive advantages, you can check the level of interest and support for the new concept while also assessing its feasibility based on the funds raised and feedback received.

5. *An early access programme.* Offer early access to your MLP to a group of interested users or customers before its official launch. This not only generates excitement and anticipation, but also provides valuable insights into user behaviour, preferences, and potential challenges. By closely monitoring early adopters' experiences and feedback, you can refine the MLP and ensure its attractiveness and feasibility align with market expectations.

The results of these five types of experiments are not only input for iterating your MLP. Assuming that you do more than one experiment, which is highly likely, the data from your experiments are a perfect bedrock to draft your innovation business case, which I will discuss in Strategy 14 to win management buy-in for change.

How much should you allocate to experimenting?

Experimenting is learning by doing. It's essential in understanding if you're on the right track. That's why it's important, especially when you work in a big organisation, to budget for experimenting big time. Check out the advice of the CTO of Hewlett Packard, in which she advises you to allocate ten per cent, at least.

You need to allocate ten per cent of your budget to experimenting [3]

As you shape your plans for the year, don't make them so rigid that you can't pivot. That's the lesson from Fidelma Russo. She is the Chief Technology Officer at Hewlett Packard Enterprise. There she drives their innovation team, working on big ideas for the future. She shared how leaders can be nimble, so they're always prioritising the most innovative ideas. She even shared how they can find the budget for them.

"In some ways, the yearly planning cycle is a good thing. In other ways, it can be somewhat stifling, and technology cycles tend not to run on yearly planning cycles. Gen AI didn't. I mean, it didn't really go according to our planning cycles. And so all of us had to adjust last year and say, what are we going to take out? And so, if I took something like GEN AI – what we've actually done is to say, okay, wasn't in our budget cycle, wasn't in our planning cycle, but we've adjusted and said in every business unit, what are you doing internally? How are you using it to change your product, and your product trajectory? What are you doing that may have been more traditional than you could accelerate. And where are the experiments that you're doing?

The other question is, how much of your budget are you allocating to experimenting? You need to be allocating about 10 per cent of your budget to that. And that seems like a lot. But there's always money in everybody's budget that's being spent on what I would call sedimentation, you know, down at the bottom. And I would encourage every leader to look and say, how do I find that money? Because if you don't find that money and use it to for things that may seem a little bit of a moonshot or a crazy idea, then you're not allowing your team to think outside the box enough and you're going to miss an opportunity."

I hope that I made it clear that to understand whether a really innovative idea is going to succeed, you have to test the experience, not just show someone a piece of paper. Experimenting de-risks innovation as it generates actual data on both attractiveness and feasibility, and that's how you win buy-in for change at your senior managers.

In the next chapter I will present a great example on experimenting at SAP, a big company where management buy-in for change was accelerated by creating a safe zone for experimentation.

Key messages from this chapter:

☞ Experimenting mitigates risks and fosters buy-in for radical change.

☞ Testing, learning, and adapting are core-activities of agile innovation teams.

☞ Create an MLP: a Minimum Loveable Product.

☞ There are many types of experiments to test both the attractiveness and feasibility.

☞ You need to allocate ten per cent of your budget to experimentation.

[1] 'How Corporate Purpose Leads to Innovation', HBR, November 01, 2023.
[2] Userpilot, https://userpilot.com/blog/minimum-delightful-product/
[3] Source: WEF. https://www.weforum.org/podcasts/meet-the-leader/episodes/leaders-should-prioritize-in-2024/

Alberto Savoia

"Test it
invest

before you in it."

CREATING A SAFE EXPERIMENTATION ZONE AT SAP

By Claus von Riegen

CONTEXT OF SAP

SAP employs more than 100,000 people globally. Can you imagine that employees are able to test drive new product ideas with customers almost as if they would run their own start-up? Let me explain how we have been able to establish such an environment – a safe experimentation zone.

For large corporations like SAP to be innovative, the biggest challenge is not a lack of creativity. Corporations have lots of talented people and a plenitude of exchanges with external stakeholders such as customers, partners, and academic institutions. Innovation in large corporations is difficult primarily for two other reasons. First, it can't be predicted which of the many ideas will result in noticeable market success. Managing – and reducing – the unavoidable uncertainty is not a skill set that commonly resides in larger corporations. And second, a truly innovative idea will sooner or later face the corporate immune system. This exists for good reason, that is, to protect and optimise the corporation's core and running business. But it's not great for supporting the creation of new businesses. *"An immune system is a system that protects an organism against diseases. It detects a wide variety of agents and distinguishes them from the organism's own healthy tissue."* Applying this in a business context means that basically anything that is different to what the corporation knows, may lead to a disease. Which is why innovation – due to it being new and different – is prevented. And for intrapreneurs, this represents a competitive disadvantage by design compared to independent start-ups that are pursuing the same market. So how can we overcome this?

SHARED PAIN POINTS

Back in 2016, I led the Business Model Innovation team at SAP that was responsible for commercialising new business models. We were part of the larger finance & administration board area and thus, reviewed all requests for new business model ideas together with stakeholders of the different functions. For example, for every new offering to be commercialised, the accounting team needed to determine the appropriate revenue recognition treatment to ensure that revenues are recognised in compliance with global accounting standards. Which in turn required a time-consuming cost structure determination and fair value calculation of the offering along with a business case with all key assumptions.

One day in the summer of that year, I met our Chief Accounting Officer at the coffee corner and told him how painful and time-consuming it is to educate his team and wait on their guidance, especially recognising that most of these new offerings were failing in the market anyway. So my question to him was: *"Why are we trying to be super accurate from an accounting perspective when there is usually no significant revenue anyway?"* To my surprise, he shared my observation – he didn't find it valuable that his team was spending time on commercialising new offerings that did not result in recognisable market success. He asked me to predict market successes better so that we can avoid wasting his team's time. I responded that that is not possible, and that we can only find out whether an offering is successful by testing it under real market conditions. Eventually, we agreed to task both our teams to design a programme for testing innovation where the standard commercialisation process would only be applied AFTER a successful test, not BEFORE. Which would help both our teams to spend time on things that really matter. Of course, this approach itself was required to be compliant with accounting standards. Therefore, we ideated a small list of boundary conditions like a revenue ceiling and a limitation in terms of number of seats on the programme to have this environment controlled in some way and off we went. The decisive element was the revenue ceiling – that is, the annual sum of the revenues of all offerings on the programme needed to be below a certain amount to be far from being material to the overall annual revenues of the SAP group (€22.1 billion in 2016). We basically invented an accounting grey zone for innovation. Or, in other words, enabled innovation to happen based on a rounding error in the group's P&L statement.

MUTUAL RESPECT

To reach this pragmatic solution on how to account for early innovations required three principles. First, to openly share and discuss the pain points that result out of the application of corporate standards (e.g., wasted efforts or long delays). Second, to develop a trusted relationship to corporate functions that are required for innovation to succeed. You need them as a partner, not as a blocker. And third, to make the corporate functions part of the innovation programme – instead of allowing them to say no to your request, ask questions in an open, almost provocative manner such as: "Under which circumstances would you support this?"

When we applied these principles along all key corporate functions, we realised that we were onto something. The establishment of a **safe experimentation zone**. A zone where intrapreneurs, that is, entrepreneurs within the corporation, can pursue their business idea almost independently from corporate constraints. We realised that for this zone to be successful, it needed to demonstrate the following principles:

Intrapreneurs
- Want to observe **psychological safety** to be allowed to fail in the pursuit of their business idea – failure is actually a common outcome and, therefore, it needs to be accepted.
- Want to be shielded from the corporate immune system so that they can pursue their business idea in a very **fast**, **flexible** and **inexpensive** manner – almost like a start-up within the corporation.

The corporation
- Wants no disruption of its core operations – for example, there must be no compromise on **compliance** with rules that are enforced legally.
- Has an interest that experiments happen in a rather **disciplined** manner – when there is failure, it should happen fast and inexpensively.

Ultimately, the goal is to minimise the disadvantages and maximise the advantages for intrapreneurs of being part of the larger corporation. At the end of the day, the funding for the intrapreneurs' experiments comes from the corporation's profitable core operations. Which is an advantage over independent start-ups that constantly need to worry about their fundraising from investors.

With the above principles we even convinced our Chief Financial Officer to sponsor our approach and motivate his teams to support it. He recognised that this safe experimentation zone was needed due to the risky nature of innovation and the otherwise cumbersome processes being applied, especially from many of the teams he was responsible for.

JOINT SOLUTION

With this sponsorship from our CFO, we went ahead and organised a workshop with senior executives from key functions across the company to solicit their buy-in to the overall idea of a safe experimentation zone. It was fascinating to observe how the attitude changed from: "no, this is not possible" to: "in this controlled environment, we can be more flexible and make it happen." The workshop was a turning point, especially given that the executives recognised that the safe experimentation zone was also helpful for them. Dropping the need for intrapreneurs to gather complex approvals or following cumbersome processes also helped their teams to spend less time and effort with such cases at early stages.

We eventually called our innovative way to innovate our 'incubation channel' and in the following years continued to further enhance its mechanics and the support provided by the various functions from across the company. Below are a few examples of the benefits that teams enjoy when utilising the incubation channel for their early-stage innovation.

Procurement
- Teams are exempted from running a request for proposal, organised by the corporate procurement team, and can select their own vendors and products if the respective procurement amount is below a certain threshold.

Hiring
- Teams can hire through their recruiting agency of choice; any corporate hiring restrictions don't apply.

Engineering
- Only legally required product qualities are to be complied with, such as product security, data protection and privacy, and licensing requirements from utilised third-party products; all other product qualities (e.g., performance, user experience, localisation) are at the full discretion of the team (and can be dropped if determined as unnecessary).

Cloud operations & support
- There is full flexibility on how to operate cloud service instances, yet compliance to corporate software delivery requirements (e.g., export control) is needed.
- There is no need to provide 24/7 enter-

prise support for customers, best effort is sufficient.

Commercialisation
-   There is no need to develop a business case and follow the standard commercialisation process, which has an idea-to-market time of several months.
-   Teams enjoy complete commercial flexibility, products can be provided free-of-charge or tested with a known or new pricing model and set of price points.
-   There is dedicated support for contract creation and finance processes such as contracting and order-to-cash from corporate legal and corporate process teams, respectively.

GtM & Sales
-   Account executives will be compensated against their sales quota towards selling products out of the incubation channel so that there is no disadvantage compared to regular products on the standard pricelist.

BENEFITS & CALL TO ACTION

Using the incubation channel, we have been able to test drive some 30+ product ideas over the past few years with customers around the globe. Many of these ideas were later discontinued and we recognised that this was also much faster and cheaper compared to standard products. At the same time, a few product ideas became true success stories that now appreciate the scale of SAP's market presence: SAP Signavio Process Insights and SAP Green Token were both started by a team of two and now contribute to our growing cloud revenue streams. In early 2017, our Chief Innovation Officer sent an email to our CEO stating: '*It took a team of four people just two months from the first line of code to our approved 'beta launch'. We look forward to sharing many such stories in the future of SAP innovating at start-up speed!*'

The incubation channel, SAP's safe experimentation zone for innovation, has demonstrated that innovation – even if being adjacent to the core business – can thrive organically. And talent does not need to leave SAP to pursue new business ideas and demonstrate their entrepreneurial skills.

Do you think this concept is useful for your organisation? Consider these five key elements of success:

1. **Secure an executive sponsor**
    In SAP's case, it was our CFO who understood that innovation, due to its new way of doing business, required a safe experimentation zone. In your case, it might be an executive with a different function, but make sure that they have the power to bend the rules as far as needed for innovation to succeed.

2. **Establish a core team taking ownership for the safe experimentation zone**
    Ideally, you bring together people that understand the needs from both the corporate functions and operations as well as the intrapreneurs to be served. We had a good experience hiring consultants that became translators and bridge builders between both worlds.

3. **Build bridges to key corporate functions**
Identify all corporate functions from which you need support. And recruit representatives from their teams to virtually join your team and spend part of their time on building and protecting the safe experimentation zone. In our case, some of the key corporate functions were legal, accounting as well as engineering and finance processes.

4. **Design service catalogue**
When designing the elements of the safe experimentation zone, you have basically three options:

a. Ignore corporate constraints that don't add value to intrapreneurs (e.g., cost structure determination and revenue recognition assessment).

b. Follow minimum corporate requirements to ensure legal compliance (e.g., data protection and privacy).

c. Borrow existing corporate services or specifically adapt them to intrapreneurs' needs (e.g., sales compensation equal to standard sales incentivisation model).

In any case, design the safe experimentation zone in a way that you consider the benefits for both, the intrapreneurs and the corporate functions.

5. **Celebrate early successes and never stop learning**
Make sure that the outcomes of the safe experimentation zone are recognised. Let the first intrapreneurs in your organisation share their appreciation of the benefits. Regularly thank the corporate functions for their support - even better if this comes from your executive sponsor.

CULURE-RELATED STRATEGY

Be a Great Innovator

IMPACTS MOST

4 CULTURAL NORMS

- -

IMPACTS ALSO

2 LACK OF DIVERSITY

7 RISK AVERSION

In the process of winning - and keeping management buy-in for your innovations - you yourself can play a huge role by being the innovation leader or facilitator. You, mastering innovation in all its aspects, must build trust and show others that you are the right person to lead the initiative.

When you are a great innovator, and stay authentic and comply to the cultural norms, you can break internal barriers because 'you are one of them'. This builds trust and understanding. And that's a good start for winning buy-in. By being a great innovator, you challenge the lack of diversity by putting it prominent on the agenda and solving this issue while composing your team. You lower the risk aversion barrier too, as your reputation will create the confidence that you will deliver strategic innovation outcomes.

The jockey and the horse

Innovation is all about ideas and innovative people. In the world of venture capital, the analogy of 'the horse and jockey' is often applied. There's a discussion amongst venture capitalists if you should say yes to an innovation business case based on the founder or start-up team, 'the jockey', or based on the new idea itself, 'the horse'.

An interesting lesson from the successful Pixar Animation Studios, was described by Ed Catmull, former president of Pixar Animation and Disney Animation. He talked to the head of a movie studio who said that his biggest problem was not finding good people but finding good ideas. Catmull's experience was exact the opposite. He experienced that if you give a top idea to a mediocre team, they will likely ruin it. But if you give a mediocre idea to a top team, they will find a way to make it work in the end.

In innovation, the jockey (you) matters just as much as the horse (idea). In my opinion, the extent to which the idea and the innovator matter differs per phase of the innovation process. At the start, the front end of innovation, the jockey might even be more important than the horse, because the idea is in such an embryonic stage, that your trust in the innovator dominates the trust in the idea. At the back end of innovation, however, the concept ready-to-be-launched has been worked out and tested on so many details that the trust in the idea might outgrow the trust in the innovation team managing it.

Of course, as 'a jockey' you must master essential 'riding capabilities', like visionary thinking, analysing market trends and customer needs, creativity and problem-solving skills, risk management, decision making, understanding financial implications, managing budgets, project management, and understanding technical aspects relevant to your innovation projects.

According to Joe Hampshire, a retired American jockey, being a jockey is more than just riding a horse. "Riding is only one part of being a jockey. Your personality, the way you present yourself, your work ethic, and the way you cope with the ups and downs of racing are the secrets to success."

The same applies for innovators leading corporate projects or start-ups. As an innovator, your personality, your soft skills and your authority make a difference in winning and keeping management buy-in for radical innovation.

To be able to win, and especially keeping management buy-in to support your innovation projects, the twelve 'riding capabilities' mentioned above form a solid base. But they are not enough. It's your soft skills that will make the difference, developing and launching new concepts on the market.

Ten Things Great Innovators Do

The past forty years, I learned how to break innovation barriers the hard way when I tried to navigate the ocean of innovation as manager, innovator, and design thinker. I would like to share ten things that successful innovators do. Ten things that will help you manoeuvre your idea through all the scepticism and resistance, towards a successful launch.

Ten Things Great Innovators Do to Win Management Buy-in		
	1. Be courageous.	6. Be persistent.
	2. Love your idea.	7. Influence hearts and minds.
	3. Be a storyteller.	8. Put your team in the spotlight.
	4. Tell your why first.	9. Make things happen.
	5. Show your will and passion.	10. Be authentic.

1. Be Courageous. Innovation requires the courage to challenge existing norms and take risks. Be bold in your vision and unafraid to pioneer new ideas. As an innovator you need to have:

- ☛ the courage to say to your top manager: "You're not going to stop me; I will do it anyway!"
- ☛ the courage to continue to work on your innovation, even when your family and friends say you should give up.
- ☛ the courage to pivot for the third time, as the first two concepts were not successful enough.
- ☛ the courage to ask for more budget if it takes longer than you expected.

Be sure to know, I admire your courage as an innovator.

2. Love Your Idea. Passion and persistence are essential ingredients for innovation. Treat your radical idea with the same dedication and care as you would your child, and fight for it.

As an innovator, you take risks and stretch your comfort zone continuously, out of love for your idea.

3. Be a Storyteller. Compelling storytelling captivate audiences and inspire action. You must craft a narrative that conveys the essence and impact of your innovation.

Stories entertain, inform, educate, inspire, and influence people. Storytelling is a great tool for persuasion. It establishes a deep emotional connection and engages the imagination. A compelling story not only conveys information, it creates a narrative that resonates with your audience's experiences and values. It's a powerful way for you to communicate complex ideas. And it's scientifically proven that stories trigger the release of oxytocin, a hormone that creates positive feelings which enhances trust, empathy, and cooperation.

4. Tell Your Why first. Be sure to start by clearly articulating the purpose and motivation behind your innovation to gain interest and support. Simon Sinek's famous TED Talk on 'Start with Why' emphasises the importance of defining the purpose of your endeavours as an innovator. By communicating the why behind your innovation, you can connect with stakeholders on a deeper level, fostering buy-in and enthusiasm. Why? Because as Sinek says, "People don't buy what you do, they buy why you do it." It's a fact of life that people are far more likely to accept a change when they understand the reason for it.

5. Show Your Will and Passion. Consistently demonstrate your commitment to realise your innovation project. I love the following quote from the famous economist Joseph Schumpeter from 1928 which reflects this perfectly. He wrote: "Successful innovation is a feat not of intellect but of will.'

6. Be persistent. Of course, you need the courage to stick out your neck to start innovation. You need the creativity to ideate new disruptive solutions. And you need the discipline to transform an idea into reality. But your most important personality trait as an innovator is your persistence. It's being persistent in transforming all the nos you get on your innovation journey into yesses, which makes you successful in the end. This is evident from a poll on LinkedIn amongst 665 professionals, with which I completely agree.

As an innovator, which personality trait made you successful?

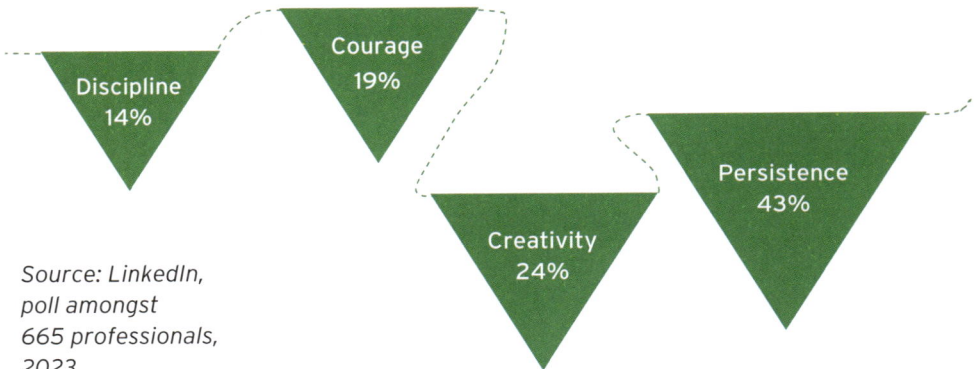

Discipline
14%

Courage
19%

Creativity
24%

Persistence
43%

Source: LinkedIn, poll amongst 665 professionals, 2023

A great example of persistency is British inventor Sir James Dyson. He made 5,127 prototypes of his famous Dual Cyclone bagless vacuum cleaner before settling on the model that would make him a billionaire.

7. Influence Hearts and Minds. I hope you recognise that the decision to start doing new things is often influenced by both emotions as well as logic. Appeal to the emotions of decision-makers by aligning your innovation with their values.

By telling stories you appeal to both logic and emotion. They help you explain complex ideas, demonstrate benefits, and create a memorable impression.

8. Put Your Team in the Spotlight. Acknowledge and celebrate the contributions of your team members, recognising that innovation is a collaborative effort. I call it we-nnovation instead of i-nnovation. Your team's culture should be cognitively diverse and psychologically safe. Also, when your team members are struggling, underperforming or just failing, protect them and take responsibility.

9. Make Things Happen. Actions speaks louder than words. Take initiative and execute your ideas to demonstrate their feasibility and potential impact. Be the champion.

10. Be Authentic. Build trust with stakeholders by embodying authenticity and integrity in all your interactions.

Besides these ten things which will help you to win management buy-in, I'd like to discuss two other relevant personal topics for innovators.

1. Innovators are equilibrists

"To innovate you have to walk as a leopard, be brave as a lion, and be agile as a gazelle." This wonderful saying of design professor Sergio Correa de Jesus really inspired me. You must be three animals, with quite contradictory characteristics, united in one person. So, you must be an equilibrist, as you must find the right balance between five aspects:

1. between the business of today and the business of tomorrow.
2. between design thinking and business thinking.
3. between your promise and your deliverable.
4. between customer interests and company interests.
5. between risks and rewards.

2. Innovators are of all ages

A lot of managers assume that establishing a culture of innovation would require bringing young people into their organisations. I tell them they are wrong.

Innovation has nothing to do with age, and everything to do with mindset. I travel all over the world giving lectures to innovators. And I observe in practice that innovation is of all ages. The view that being an innovator has nothing to do with age is also supported by research of Benjamin Jones of Northwestern University. He states that a 55-year-old and even a 65-year-old, has significantly more innovation potential than a 25-year-old. He based his conclusions on data on Nobel Prize winners and great inventors.

In conclusion, a real innovator is a curious, creative, courageous, convincing, disciplined, and persistent human being. By internalising the ten things I mentioned in this chapter, as a great innovator, you can effectively win management buy-in, creating a culture for innovation for yourself and your organisation.

Now you might be ready to innovate. But is it really the right moment for the market and your organisation too? Check it out in the next chapter: Seize the innovation sweet spot.

Key messages from this chapter:

☞ People say yes because of the jockey or because of the horse.

☞ Storytelling is a great tool for persuasion.

☞ Innovation has nothing to do with age, but with mindset.

☞ Your soft skills and your personality make the difference.

Gijs van Wulfen

"Innovation starts at the end of your comfort zone."

7 Seize the Innovation Sweet Spot

IMPACTS MOST

12 NO PRIORITY TO INNOVATE

IMPACTS ALSO

4 CULTURAL NORMS

9 SHORT-TERM FOCUS

Seizing the innovation sweet spot helps you to get radical innovation prioritised at senior management. Picking the right moment helps to break the conservative cultural norms and creates momentum to shift the focus from the short term to the future.

Most of the time, continuous innovation is on senior management's agenda

Most organisations, even the most conservative, innovate continuously, at least that's what they claim. You can define continuous innovation as an ongoing process of introducing new ideas, products, services or business models to drive growth and profits. Continuous innovation focuses on making incremental improvements and adaptations over time. It's more about better ideas than new ideas, like radical innovation.

Now, don't get me wrong: There's nothing wrong with incremental innovation. As a business economist, I am very much aware that this type of innovation of small steps and little risks is essential in keeping profits up to standard.

When you look at how companies spend their innovation budgets, there's no wonder that incremental innovation is leading; 58 per cent of R&D spending is directed at incremental innovations, 28 per cent at substantial innovations, and only 14 per cent at radical innovations [1]. Companies tend to prefer incremental innovations in small steps over radical innovations in big jumps, as they can be implemented faster with less perceived risk and less resources needed.

So how can you win management buy-in for radical innovation and get it prioritised?

Two sweet spots for radical innovation

An important reason why few radical innovations hit the market is that senior managers are risk averse. Most of us, your leaders as well, will pursue and approve radical innovations only when we are aware that lower-risk concepts cannot generate any real growth and extra profits anymore. I'd like to quote the CEO of BMW AG, the German luxury car producer, Dr Norbert Reithofer. When asked why BMW started the risky E-car project with the BMWi-3 and i-8, he responded very honest: "Because doing nothing was an even bigger risk". [2]

To be effective as an innovator, these are the moments you should look out for. A seasoned innovator in a large organisation acts with the patience of a hunter:

"When it comes to taking a shot, take your time. Remember that most hunters, even very experienced ones, have no business trying a shot at a running animal. All too often doing so results in a wounded deer that is never recovered. Wait for a shot that you're sure you can make."

But you're faced with a dilemma. You can't wait too long. You know completion of the innovation process in a big company takes on average at least 18 – 36 months from the idea to introducing it to the market. And in many industrial sectors even longer. So it is extremely important to anticipate and (re)act on time. Leaks in the roof are easy to spot when it's raining, but it's better to have the repairs done beforehand. The innovation process can only succeed if the company is financially and mentally sound enough to do this. In the middle of a crisis when the board of directors and your co-workers are under a lot of pressure, you should think twice before starting an innovation project. It's best to wait until the dust has settled.

So pick one of the two sweet spots for innovation: the moment you want to innovate, or the moment you need to innovate.

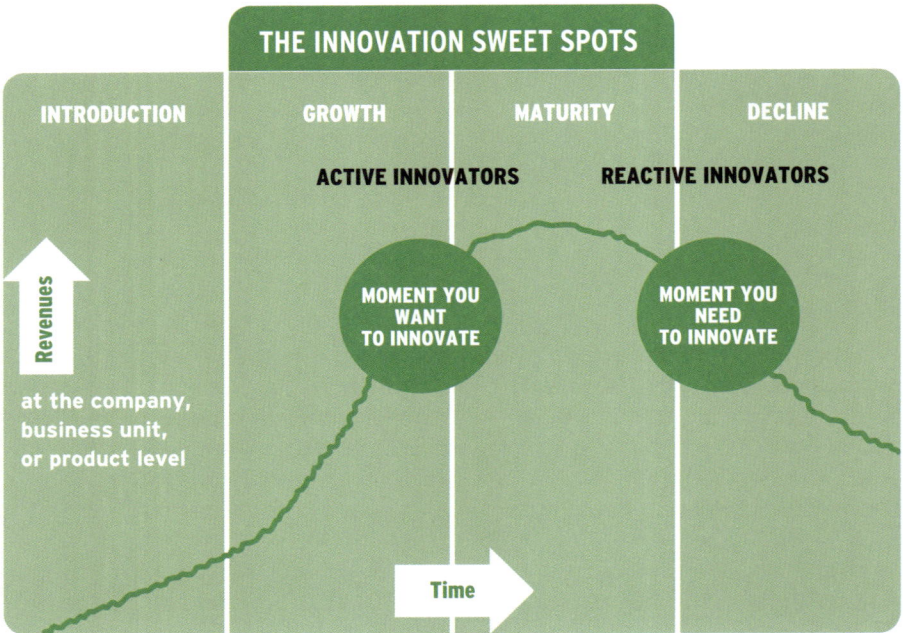

THE INNOVATION SWEET SPOTS

INTRODUCTION   GROWTH   MATURITY   DECLINE

ACTIVE INNOVATORS   REACTIVE INNOVATORS

Revenues at the company, business unit, or product level

MOMENT YOU WANT TO INNOVATE

MOMENT YOU NEED TO INNOVATE

Time

The moment you want to innovate radically out of ambition

In practice, I see organisations approach radical innovation in two different ways: those who want to innovate and those who need to innovate. I call those who want to innovate the active innovators and the ones who need to innovate the passive innovators. As you can see in the figure, their roles are defined by when they really innovate their business. Every organisation, business unit or product has its lifecycle of introduction, growth, maturity and decline. Active innovators, who want to innovate in a radical way, give innovation priority at the end of the growth stage. They want to innovate before they reach maturity, often for several reasons simultaneously:

- ☛ To keep their revenue stream growing;
- ☛ To maintain an innovative mindset;
- ☛ To boost internal entrepreneurship (intrapreneurship);
- ☛ To address changing needs and wants of customers;
- ☛ To lead in technology;
- ☛ To expand their business by new business models, distribution channels and customer groups;
- ☛ To anticipate on new governmental regulations or a market liberalisation.

A great way to win management buy-in for radical innovation for active innovators is to align innovation to strategy, which I will show you in the next chapter.

The moment you need to innovate radically out of necessity

Reactive innovators, on the contrary, wait. They wait until they get hit by a crisis, their markets saturate or get disrupted by new technologies and/or business models. They reorganise, lay-off people and prioritise innovation only at the start of their stage of decline when they need to innovate radically out of necessity. They need to innovate most often with only one goal in mind: to stop revenues and profits from dropping and build a new future for their organisation.

And in the meantime?

So how can you try and break the status quo and create momentum for radical innovation? Of course, Strategy 2, cultivating innovation ambassadors, will help you a lot. You create an informal structure of innovation ambassadors, who help you to prioritise innovation at key decision makers.

As senior managers will only radically innovate out of necessity, your challenge is to make them nervous that doing nothing is indeed a big risk. How? By understanding your managers' agenda (Strategy 1), identifying the key decision makers on innovation, and to confront them personally with concrete reasons for change that will move them out of their comfort zone.

So how can you move your senior managers out of their comfort zone?
- ☞ Take them to visit trendy start-ups that are challenging your position.
- ☞ Invite a trendwatcher to confront them with how quick the world is changing.
- ☞ Visit ex-customers who just switched to a very innovative competitor.
- ☞ Take them to Tech Universities to experience new virtual reality and AI technologies.
- ☞ Show great examples from leading countries applying new AI solutions.
- ☞ Spam them with articles of new successful business models.
- ☞ Visit young customers and ask what they think of your brand and products.

Your conservative managers will say yes to radical innovation as soon as they get the insight themselves that doing nothing is an even bigger risk, as necessity is the mother of invention.

In the next chapter you will read the Innovation Story of a business unit of Huntsman, a chemical company from the USA, and how they picked the right moment to innovate in EAME (Europe - Asia - Middle East) with Thermoplastic Polyurethanes. After that, I will show how you how to align innovation to strategy to win buy-in for radical change.

Key-messages from this chapter:

☞ Continuous innovation focuses on making incremental improvements.

☞ There are two sweet spots for radical innovation.

☞ There's a moment you want to innovate radically out of ambition.

☞ The moment you need to innovate radically out of necessity.

☞ Make senior managers nervous that doing nothing is a bigger risk.

[1] Source. www.innovationexcellence.com/
blog/2014/10/28/the-2014-global-innovation-
1000-study-from-strategy/
[2] Dutch car magazine, *Autoweek*, 41-2013.

Gijs van Wulfen

"An innovator
patience of a
the right

should have the hunter to pick moment."

HOW TO PICK THE RIGHT MOMENT TO INNOVATE AT HUNTSMAN

By Denis Turmel [1]

In 2013, as Market Sector Expert for the European Business Development Team of Huntsman Polyurethanes, I was assigned to look at different methodologies to boost innovation. The European Business Development Team was responsible to tackle all non-core innovation opportunities from a technical and marketing viewpoint. At the time, Huntsman was a manufacturer of differentiated chemical products with a revenue of around $10 billion and 10,000 employees. It offered a broad range of chemicals and formulations, such as amines, isocyanates, epoxies, textile chemicals and dyes.

In my investigations, while I was looking for proven innovation methodologies, I encountered about twenty innovation methodologies and service providers which offered potential: some large well-known global consulting firms and other smaller boutique innovation firms. I discovered one of them at an evening organised by the European Young Innovators Forum in Brussels in the summer of 2013.

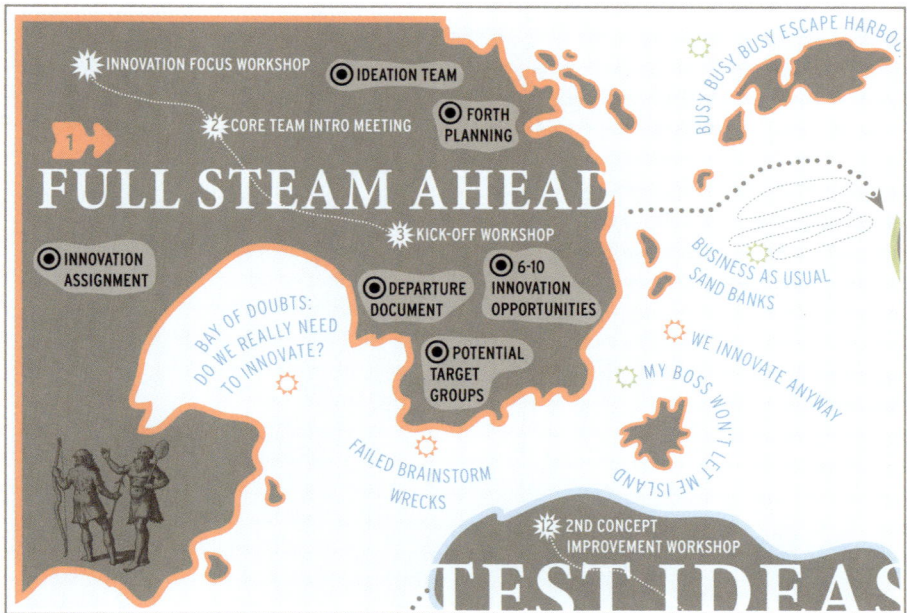

FORTH innovation method step 1: Full Steam Ahead (see page 67).

DISCOVERING A NEW METHODOLOGY

That evening, we were with about thirty keen innovators eager to get inspired and learn new, effective ways to innovate. It was the moment I discovered FORTH, a front end innovation methodology developed by Gijs Van Wulfen. Gijs arrived with his famous innovation expedition map and easel under his arm to present FORTH. Unlike many other methods I was exploring, FORTH was simple, easy to communicate and well-timed. As there were no royalties or fees to implement it yourself, it could be subsequently used independently by companies. FORTH is an acronym made of the letters describing the five steps of the method: 1) Full steam ahead; 2) Observe & learn; 3) Raise ideas; 4) Test ideas; 5) Homecoming. It delivers so-called mini new business cases supported by senior leadership, which are ready to enter the product development funnel. FORTH was a major exercise for an organisation, as it was running over six months and engaging a core team of six to ten employees, with senior leaders also attending major stages of the process. It was not a quick win: it was to be used to fundamentally change the way companies innovate, as well as to change their culture.

THRILLED TO START OUR INNOVATION JOURNEY

I remember vividly how thrilled I was by the potential of implementing the FORTH method at Huntsman. Finally, I had found a method that transformed the fuzzy front end into easy to follow steps, and combined creativity with structure, offering tangible outcomes after each step. As Gijs always says: "It combined Design Thinking with business thinking", which was what was mostly missing at that time. The method also offered the potential to bring together multifunctional teams, typically not directly involved in innovation, but this time fully engaged in it. This broad engagement across the whole organisation was creating innovation ambassadors or godparents to the method and, most importantly, to the mini new business cases and the innovation culture. That evening in Brussels marked the start of my effective journey as innovation facilitator!

NO PRIORITY WHEN FOCUSED ON EFFICIENCY

In the first half of 2014, I connected with Gijs, the founder of the FORTH innovation method, and the two of us organised a first workshop with some subject matter experts and decision makers (business and technical directors) at Huntsman polyurethanes headquarters in Brussels. The presentation was very well received with keen interest from several people, but... nothing happened. So we decided to organise another session in the second half of 2014. Unfortunately, it had the same outcome: nothing happened.

At that time, Huntsman was going through a major reorganisation in the EAME region. Though there was a sense of urgency to change the game in innovation, priority was given to both operational and commercial excellence. In other words, continue operational improvements as we always did, but by extracting any potential optimisation opportunities. It became clear to me that it was not the right time to invest in a major innovation exercise. As frustrating as this was for me personally, I learned an important lesson too: companies do not launch ambitious innovation programmes when focus is on efficiency.

PICKING THE RIGHT MOMENT

The story continues though. In 2015, I was invited to lead marketing for another business unit of Huntsman in EAME: Thermoplastic Polyurethanes (TPU). The TPU business was global, led by a visionary and charismatic vice president who had been creating double digit growth in both volume and value since 2012. This growth had essentially been achieved via share-shift using Huntsman high-quality TPU products.

One year into my role, the leadership and I were reviewing our performance: the business remained healthy, margins were good, we were innovating, but innovations were essentially product tweaks for single customers. We had reached our fair share in many market segments and our existing innovation funnel was not going to support our growth ambitions sufficiently. I said to the president of Elastomers: "Unless we fundamentally transform the way we innovate; we will continue to just do incremental innovation". With the support of a visionary leader and a sense of urgency, the moment seemed right to suggest a thorough innovation journey aiming for more radical innovations which could move the proverbial needle. In December 2016, our vice president agreed for us to present the FORTH innovation method, which I was chosen to guide, to the leadership team (directors of Sales, Marketing, Operation, HR, Finance, Technology & Supply Chain). Our goal: to gain their support and secure the necessary resources. I was thrilled by broad support to initiate the innovation process. Finally, I pitched FORTH innovation at the right moment. From that point onwards, the ball started rolling quickly.

GETTING READY TO START

In March 2017, we started the FORTH innovation journey via the first step of the process: the Innovation Focus Workshop. Over the course of one morning, we wrote the innovation assignment, chose the cross-functional core team and pencilled-in the other fourteen workshops to come. We were amazed by the efficiency of the process! Our vice president, technology director, marketing director and two other senior colleagues who were present agreed to move forward.

I felt genuine commitment to the six-month innovation process: I was going to co-facilitate the first FORTH innovation journey for Huntsman with Gijs, its founder. The FORTH innovation facilitator training was starting in April in Lettele, a tiny village near Deventer, the Netherlands. An entire new story could be written about this memorable training, during which the six-month programme was condensed into one week, where through case studies and role play, we went through the whole FORTH expedition.

THE JOURNEY DELIVERED

The FORTH kick-off was set for September 2017, so we had four months to prepare: visit and rent inspiring venues for the main workshops; connect to each team member to explain the journey; prepare the supporting communication material to help the global

TPU community follow the FORTH innovation journey along its five steps; and define a detailed programme for each workshop. In September that year, nineteen people were present for our official FORTH innovation kick-off: the vice president, director of Sales/Technology/Marketing, the core team (nine), the extended team (four), and Gijs and myself as co-facilitators. Later in the process, we also invited participants from other business units to get new insights and communicate on FORTH using hands-on engagement.

Six months later, we had six mini new business cases for radical innovation projects, which we collectively rated at the end presentation. Four mini new business cases were selected to become actual projects in our stage-gated innovation process. They were resourced adequately, thanks to the engagement of senior leaders at all key steps of the FORTH process. Each person on the extended team of leaders became godparent to one of the innovation projects selected; this was instrumental to success.

Jan Verstraeten - VP,
Global Elastomers

"From the very start, the FORTH innovation process turned out to be an exciting adventure with, maybe a bit to my surprise, steady and visible progress all throughout the process. Next to having delivered on its promises, the methodology served as a catalyst to instigate innovative thinking throughout the organisation. The fact that this innovation expedition was performed by a broad cross-section of the organisation, rather than simply technologists and marketing people, was instrumental in achieving that."

A CULTURE FOR INNOVATION

In addition to delivering six cases for radical innovation, the FORTH innovation process contributed to initiate a major innovation culture change in TPU. FORTH was a major growth opportunity and learning experience for each participant. Afterwards both participants and their co-workers realised that innovation requires contributions and teamwork from all functions. The FORTH innovation process became TPU's front end innovation method and during the time I was still with Huntsman, FORTH was replicated with our APAC team, showing that the method worked in a very different culture like China as well. Subsequently, the regional vice president from the larger polyurethane division also selected FORTH to boost innovation in EAME. In hindsight, I realised that having initiated the FORTH innovation methodology first in a smaller, more agile business unit like TPU and having demonstrated its value, had been instrumental to leverage it to the much larger polyurethane division.

MAJOR LESSONS LEARNT

My major lesson learned as an innovator is to pick the right moment, when the soil is fertile, to drop your innovation seed. Also, start small in a more agile and open business unit, and then leverage to the larger, more conservative units.

Today I realise, in a different role for a different company, that I still use a lot of FORTH innovation tools, templates and best practices in one way or another. FORTH has been one of the most striking and enriching experiences in my professional life. At the time of writing this, I am actually preparing to introduce FORTH to my new company.

[1] Denis Turmel endorses FORTH by expressing his personal opinions while acting in his personal capacity. Mr Turmel did not author this writing as a representative of the Huntsman Corporation or its affiliates. Mr Turmel's endorsement is neither co-written, co-authored, nor endorsed by Huntsman or its affiliates.

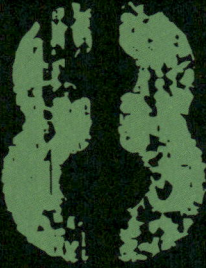

Align Innovation to Strategy

IMPACTS MOST

13 NO CLEAR DIRECTION TO INNOVATE

- -

IMPACTS ALSO

1 HISTORICAL SUCCESSES

8 RESISTANCE TO CHANGE

Aligning innovation to strategy sounds complicated, but it's not. And I am going to show you here how to facilitate it. It's a super effective strategy, because by aligning innovation to strategy you make innovation relevant for your leaders. And when you do it explicitly with an innovation assignment, you'll create a clear direction where innovation should take your organisation. You will also transform the mindset of managers by looking back to historical successes and by looking forward again to what a bright future might look like for your organisation. It will help you break the resistance to change too, as there's a great strategic reason for it.

Innovation can play a crucial role in every strategy

I hope your organisation has an inspiring mission and a clear corporate strategy. The words 'innovative, new, radical, leading, and disrupting' are probably mentioned more than once. But HOW are we going to get there? That's often an unanswered question. And that's why you should align innovation with strategy, so you can get specific about how innovation delivers compelling, feasible strategic outcomes.

Because innovation stands for *'transforming new ideas into reality with impact'*, it won't surprise you that innovation fits every strategy you can think of. I will prove it by sharing fifteen different innovation assignments for all kind of well-known strategies below:

1. *Cost Leadership*: Focuses on becoming the lowest-cost producer in the sector to gain a competitive advantage. When cost leadership is your strategy, your innovation assignment might focus on 'generating innovative ways to reduce costs by fifty per cent in five years in a sustainable way, making us the cost leader in our niche'.

2. *Differentiation*: Strives to create unique products or services that are valued by customers and are perceived as distinct from competitors. When differentiation is your strategy, your innovation assignment might focus on 'generating radical new unique offerings which will wow our customers and increase our market share with twenty per cent in the upcoming three years'.

3. *Focus Strategy*: Concentrates on serving a specific segment of the market exceptionally well, either through cost leadership or differentiation. When focus is your strategy, your innovation assignment might focus on 'generating radical new unique offerings for multiple niches which will wow our customers fitting their needs exceptionally well, outperforming all competitors in added value or price'.

4. *Vertical Integration*: Involves expanding into different stages of the supply chain to gain control over inputs or distribution channels. When vertical integration is your strategy, your innovation assignment might focus on 'generating radical new ways to dominate our supply chain within three years'.

5. *Diversification*: Spreads risk by entering new markets or industries that are unrelated to the company's current offerings. When diversification is your strategy, your innovation assignment might focus on 'generating new entries in other markets and industries with our existing or new offerings which will de-risk our company's future considerably within three years'.

6. *Market Penetration*: Focuses on increasing market share within existing markets through aggressive pricing, promotion, or distribution strategies. When market penetration is your strategy, your innovation assignment might focus on 'generating new radical ways to double our market share from fifteen to thirty per cent in three years, maintaining our present net profitability'.

7. *Market Development*: Involves entering new markets with existing products or services to expand the customer base. When market development is your strategy, your innovation assignment might focus on 'generating new growing easy-to-access markets with great potential for our current offerings to grow revenues with fifteen per cent the upcoming three years'.

8. *Sustainability Strategy*: Integrates environmental, social, and governance (ESG) principles into business operations to create long-term value and mitigate risks. When sustainability is your strategy, your innovation assignment might focus on 'generating new radical a hundred per cent sustainable green offerings for our present product/market combinations, which will generate thirty per cent of our revenues in five years'.

9. *Market Segmentation*: Divides the market into distinct groups of customers with similar needs and preferences, allowing for tailored marketing strategies. When market segmentation is your strategy, your innovation assignment might focus on 'generating new niches of customers with great profit potential within our present markets and generating new unique offerings for them leading to a twenty per cent increase of our net profits in three years'.

10. *Brand Extension*: Expands the company's brand into new product categories or markets to leverage existing brand equity. When brand extension is your strategy, your innovation assignment might focus on 'generating new growth opportunities, extending our brand into new categories co-creating new unique offerings with innovation partners doubling our sales revenues in five years'.

11. *Operational Excellence*: Focuses on improving internal processes, efficiency, and productivity to reduce costs and enhance quality. When operational excellence is your strategy, your innovation assignment might focus on 'generating new radical ways to reduce costs with ten per cent per year, each of the upcoming three years'.

12. *Customer Relationship Management (CRM)*: Emphasises building and maintaining strong relationships with customers through personalised interactions and customer service. When CRM is your strategy, your innovation assignment might focus on 'generating new radical ways to intensify customer relationships creating mutual value, increasing customer's profitability with ten per cent each year'.

13. *Customer Retention Strategy*: Focuses on keeping existing customers satisfied and loyal through loyalty programmes, rewards, and personalised offerings. When customer retention is your strategy, your innovation assignment might focus on 'generating new radical ways to retain customers, reducing customer churn from thirty per cent to ten per cent in three years'.

14. *Product Development Strategy*: Focuses on creating new or improved products to meet changing customer demands and gain a competitive edge. When product development is your strategy, your innovation assignment might focus on 'generating radical new products with a sustainable competitive advantage to revolutionise our current markets which will grow sales revenues with fifty per cent in five years'.

15. *Digital Transformation*: Focuses on leveraging digital technologies to transform business processes, operations, and customer experiences to stay competitive in the digital age. When digital transformation is your strategy, your innovation assignment might focus on 'generating radical new digital solutions creating unique offerings which will take our business processes and customer value to the next level in three years, increasing revenues and profits with thirty per cent'.

As you might have noticed, each innovation assignment has a clear direction, a quantified goal, and a specific timing. This way, you make innovation explicit and relevant as an enabler of (one of the pillars of) your (corporate) strategy.

A new CEO and a new strategy create opportunities to prioritise innovation

As discussed in Strategy 7, seizing the right moment is essential. The last twenty years that I worked as an innovation facilitator, organisations that reached out to me to help them, have approached me in two ways:

"Gijs, business is going bad, so we need to innovate. Can you help us please…?"
Those were the organisations who needed to innovate. Who understood after two cost reductions, doing the same things with less people was not going to save the company.

"Gijs, we have great new ambitions and want to innovate. Can you help us please…?"
Those were the organisations that often had changed CEO and took on a new strategy full of ambition for growth.

Especially the moments when a new CEO takes over or when a new corporate strategy is presented create great opportunities to win management buy-in for innovation. The new plans are always pivoting the original strategy with a new elan and full of ambition. And you as innovator can play a huge role delivering new radical solutions empowering the organisation to move in the chosen new direction.

That's the moment to prioritise innovation and help your leadership drafting a concrete innovation assignment in what I call an innovation focus workshop.

How to draft an innovation assignment

The innovation focus workshop is a four-hour workshop with senior managers, which I have facilitated over fifty times in the past twenty years. It's been valued highly as it converts a vague "we need to innovate" into a concrete assignment, including criteria in four hours winning buy-in from all senior managers that are present.

I have founded this technique as start of the FORTH innovation methodology, to help organisations give innovation a clear direction. It's used even before the start of the innovation process itself to make clear what the desired outcomes of an innovation process should be. The innovation focus workshop involves five steps in which the main decision makers on innovation formulate the why, what, who, where, when and which for an upcoming strategic innovation project. The typical outcome is a straightforward innovation assignment also containing the criteria that the new concepts must meet to be chosen for development and launch. The innovation assignment serves as a North Star for the innovation journey to come. The main takeaway of the innovation focus workshop is a clear understanding of the goals and deliverables of an innovation process by both the decisionmakers and the innovation team. I share with you a concrete example of an assignment for CCI, a manufacturer of sweets in the Netherlands.

Innovation assignment of CCI, a manufacturer of sweets in the Netherlands

---

"At CCI, we innovate'to make a difference'.

Because we want to be

proud, relevant,

and valuable to ensure our continuity,

with respect for people and the environment.

Therefore, we seek to ideate five new innovation business cases for evolutionary and revolutionary products, services, channels, usage methods, production techniques, or materials for end users (in the broadest sense of the word) in 'sweet moments' in Northwest Europe with galactic potential."

Of the five innovation business cases to be delivered, at least three are revolutionary, i.e., new to the respective market.

For confidentiality reasons, the quantitative criteria for each of the new business cases, which are normally part of the assignment, could not be shared with you.

The challenge for you is to get your senior managers together for an innovation workshop. By relating it to delivering strategic outcomes, you will get their attention. Why? Because in companies, attaining their strategic outcomes is personally relevant to them according to their own performance criteria for their yearly bonusses.

A full story of how innovation aligns to and supports a new strategy, you can find in the next chapter: the Innovation Story of a mid-sized company called CCI, a manufacturer of sweets in the Netherlands.

Key-messages from this chapter:

☞ By aligning innovation to strategy, you make innovation relevant for your leaders.

☞ Innovation fits every corporate strategy you can think of.

☞ A new CEO and a new strategy create opportunities to prioritise innovation.

☞ An innovation assignment creates a clear direction and deliverables.

Unknown

"There are no old roads to new destinations."

SWEET SUCCESS: CCI'S TRANSFORMATION INTO A SUSTAINABLE CONFECTIONERY PIONEER

By Rody Vonk

In Drachten, in the north of the Netherlands, you can find the headquarters of CCI – Candy Creating Impact. CCI produces sweets for consumers (both food, non-food, online retailers, and drugstores) in Europe. It also supplies its products to importers and resellers.

Over the years, CCI has developed into an innovative and sustainable company in the confectionery industry. After a significant reorganisation in 2019, it reached a crucial point in its history. It was an opportune moment to critically examine the existing strategy and invest in an approach that would prepare the company for the future. This included the decision to invest in an innovation programme to develop new, relevant, and future-proof innovative business cases.

CHANGE IN MANAGEMENT TYPE AND STRATEGY

The development the company shifted from crisis management to transformational management. This entails that CCI evolved from a 'reactive' company (that responds to urgent, often critical challenges) to an approach where the focus is on long-term change and growth. Instead of solely addressing acute issues, the company focused on redefining the organisational structure, culture, and strategies, aiming to foster sustainable development and innovation. This required a cultural shift within the organisation at all levels, as involvement was necessary from management to the shop floor to shape the future of the company.

A change was also initiated at the strategic level. Until 2019, CCI's strategy focused on cost leadership and maintaining strong customer relationships. Cost leadership means that a company strives to be the cheapest producer in its industry to gain a larger market share. This requires efficiency, strict cost management, and often investments in production capacity. Innovation was entrusted to Research & Development and primarily involved developing new products in direct response to customer requests. Thus, innovation was reactive and focused more on development, not research. Although this enabled the company to meet the immediate needs of its customers, it limited its ability to proactively innovate and respond to broader societal trends. It was clear that CCI's approach to innovation and strategy needed a new direction that focused more on creating value and less on euros and kilograms.

URGENCY FOR REAL INNOVATION

CCI realised that it was necessary to create more value and focus less solely on volume and costs. The need to develop a more valuable and sustainable business model was underscored by the need for a more positive social and ecological impact; there was a clear urgency to change the strategy.

In 2021, CCI therefore decided to embark on a journey guided by the FORTH innovation method. The choice for this approach was partly made based on the positive experiences of a contact from the network of Alfred Attema, CEO of CCI, Oscar Dekkers from Bruil. That company developed 3D concrete printing empowered by the FORTH method. Moreover, discussions with the founder of the method, Gijs van Wulfen, showed that FORTH aligned

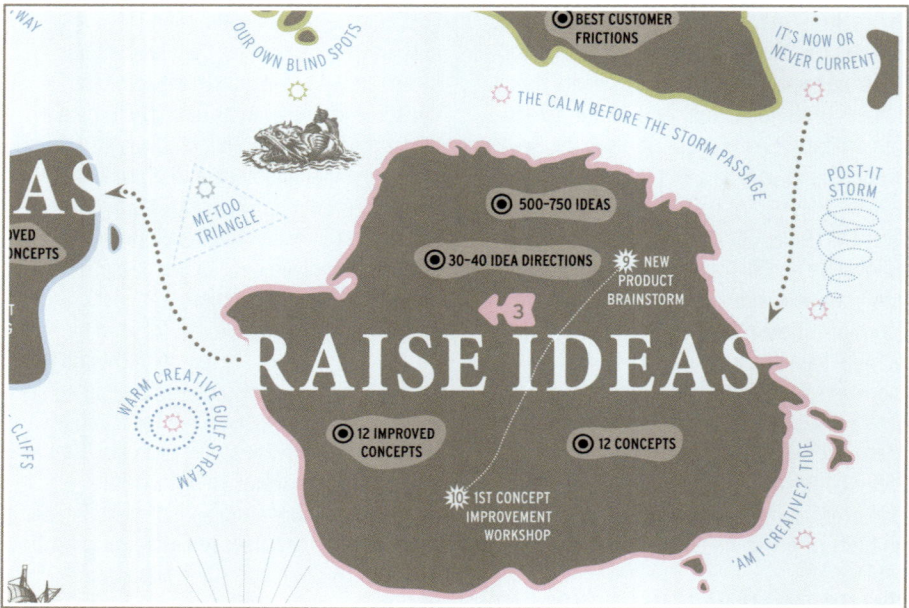

FORTH innovation method step 3: Raise Ideas (see page 67)

well with the company culture and the need for a structured process that allows for radical development without thinking too quickly in terms of solutions. The approach and philosophy of the FORTH method also aligned well with the values and objectives of CCI.

The decision to embark on the FORTH innovation method marked a turning point for CCI. It was an acknowledgment of the need to give innovation a more prominent place in the company's strategy, with the idea of not only developing new business cases, but also making a positive impact on the environment and society. This meant that from that point on, CCI's focus was not only on developing new products but also on reconsidering its business model and strategic goals.

PERSEVERANCE IS KEY

One of the key aspects for successful innovation is perseverance. Having the belief that something is possible and doing everything to make it happen. CCI's management certainly did not lack in this area.

In early March 2021, the four-month FORTH journey began. It did not start as planned, as the Netherlands was at the tail end of the COVID-19 pandemic. There was a question of whether the journey could start, especially since Gijs – one of the process facilitators – lived abroad and could not travel due to the pandemic. A so-called hybrid approach was chosen; participants were physically present in a venue and collaborated on an online whiteboard platform via their own laptops. Gijs was present via a video call, supported by a physically present second facilitator (me). This hybrid form ensured that should a participant need to quarantine during the process, they could still participate in the sessions via a video call.

When the innovation journey was about three weeks underway, the team faced another huge setback: the factory hall at CCI's main headquarters in Drachten burned down to the ground. The company management naturally had their hands full with all the arrangements that come with such a disaster. Did they still have time for a full innovation journey? Were their heads in the right place? And what did the fire mean for strategic choices to be made?

Within two weeks after the fire, the decision was made: the FORTH innovation journey had to continue! The fire also offered new perspectives. With the reconstruction of the factory, considerations and requirements for production lines that would result from new product ideas developed during the FORTH journey could be taken into account.

MANAGEMENT BUY-IN FOR INNOVATION DUE TO PARTICIPATION

Perseverance is not the only thing needed for successful innovation. A major barrier to innovation in many organisations is the lack of management buy-in. At CCI, the buy-in from key decision-makers was obtained by actively involving them in the innovation process. Some shareholders and several members of the Supervisory Board participated in several crucial workshops during the FORTH process. This approach is one of the highlights of this method, which partly makes this approach twice as successful as other methods.

At CCI, investors and management were actively involved in the FORTH journey by participating in various sessions, thereby gaining confidence in the potential of the journey. The urgency for innovation was felt, and consensus was reached on the necessity of the investment. The decision to embark on this innovation journey was seen as a necessary step for the future growth and development of the company.

THE INNOVATION TEAM FROM MULTIPLE DEPARTMENTS

Despite the so-called 'core team' that was to go through the journey having to adjust to their regular way of working in innovation, the FORTH journey got off to a good start. The fact that the team was carefully composed and had representations from various important departments of CCI meant that understanding arose for each other's perspectives and insights. A crucial condition for success! This prevents ideas from being dismissed too quickly: ultimately, ideas become everyone's, which creates support for their realisation.

THE INNOVATION ASSIGNMENT PLAYS A CRUCIAL ROLE

Good results are only achieved if you have a clear starting point. Based on the new business strategy, an innovation assignment was formulated. This is the point on the horizon that the innovation team works towards throughout the process, and it is also constantly used as a benchmark to check if the team is on the right track.

CCI created the following innovation assignment:

"At CCI, we innovate 'to make a difference.' Because we want to be proud, relevant, and valuable to ensure our continuity, with respect for people and the environment.

Therefore, we seek evolutionary and revolutionary products, services, channels, usage methods, production techniques, or materials for end users (in the broadest sense of the word) in 'sweet moments' in Northwest Europe with galactic potential.

Of the five mini new business cases (MNBCs) to be delivered, at least three are revolutionary, i.e., new to the respective market."

For confidentiality reasons, the quantitative criteria for each of the new business cases, which are normally part of the assignment, could not be shared with you.

RESULTS

The impact of the FORTH trajectory on CCI has been comprehensive. The most significant outcome was the development of the business case 'Sweets for All': vegan products that are free from the fourteen main allergens, making them edible for everyone, regardless of diet or religious background. By the end of 2024, CCI's product line of Sweets for All will be 70 per cent vegan. In addition, the company has made significant progress in sustainability, such as drastically reducing CO_2 emissions and striving for B Corp certification – a distinction awarded to companies that not only aim for profit, but also uphold a high standard of social and environmental performance, transparency, and accountability. It's a first in the industry. These efforts have not only contributed to a more sustainable business operation but have also strengthened CCI's reputation as an innovative and socially responsible enterprise.

Moreover, the FORTH journey has had a significant positive influence on the company culture at CCI. A shift has taken place towards a more proactive and forward-thinking organisation. The emphasis on innovation, sustainability, and social impact has led to a strong team spirit and a shared vision among the staff, making CCI not only a leader in the confectionery industry, but also a role model for companies striving for a positive impact on society and the environment. This is underscored by the four pillars under the new strategy and the so-called Impact Business Model that CCI is currently rolling out:

1. Having a valuable business case for the continuity of the company and its customers.

2. Being the best regional workplace, with initiatives such as bicycle plans for

employees, sleep workshops, sleep coaches, dietary workshops, preventive medical examinations, health and financial coaching, and an employee survey to measure satisfaction.

3. Creating a positive social footprint by being socially and societally active, allocating a certain percentage of EBITDA to social grants, and developing products accessible to everyone, including the implementation of the business case Sweets for All.

4. No pressure on the planet, where there is an emphasis on environmental protection and sustainability, addressing three of the United Nations Sustainable Development Goals, with a significant reduction in CO_2 emissions as one of the results.

FROM A REACTIVE COMPANY TO A MARKET PIONEER

By innovating with FORTH, CCI has proven that it is possible to be successful in the competitive confectionery market by innovating with a clear purpose in mind and following a clear process. The company has not only transformed its product offerings but has also set a new standard for what it means to be a socially responsible enterprise in the 21st century. CCI's journey from a traditional manufacturer of sweets to a pioneer in sustainable and inclusive confections offers valuable insights for other companies striving to increase their impact while meeting the needs of the modern consumer.

In a time when consumers increasingly value sustainability, health, and inclusivity, CCI has demonstrated that it is possible to integrate these values into every aspect of business operations, from product development to strategic planning. By continually striving for improvement and innovation, CCI has not only made a positive impact on the planet and the community but also laid a strong foundation for future growth and success. The transformation of CCI underscores the importance of innovation, not only as a means for commercial success but also as an instrument for positive social and ecological change.

Showcase Innovation Successes

IMPACTS MOST

7 RISK AVERSION

IMPACTS ALSO

3 FEAR OF FAILURE

8 RESISTANCE TO CHANGE

Risk aversion, the tendency to avoid or minimise risks, is a huge barrier for innovation for all of us. I will show you how showcasing innovation successes helps you break this barrier. Because showcasing innovation successes will give senior managers data-driven quantitative proof, it will help you overcome their emotional fear of failure too, and thereby diminish the resistance to change.

The origin of risk aversion of managers at companies

Why are managers in large hierarchical organisations so risk-averse? The main reasons are that corporate incentives and control processes actively discourage managers from taking risks [1]. Many large organisations even have departments or teams to identify and mitigate risks, like financial risk, operational risk, compliance risks, cybersecurity risks, and more. Avoiding or minimising risks, even if it means sacrificing potential gains, is often the preferred and rewarded behaviour. And this behaviour affects the attitude towards innovation.

Consider how most innovation decisions are made in big companies. An innovation team with an idea puts together an innovation business case to start the project at the front end of their stage-gated development process. It needs to get official approval by an innovation steering board of senior managers. The innovation leader explains the new concept, how it fits the company's strategy, and how it will benefit their customers, and the organisation. Of course, he or she also provides a financial model of the business value it will create. The innovation steering board decides based on whether it judges the strategic and financial benefits and their underlying assumptions to be plausible.

The senior managers making the decisions to invest in this innovation project will be held accountable for their innovation outcomes too. When this project does not deliver the forecasted results, their reputation, or possibly even their jobs, would be at risk. As you see, the consequences of innovation project failure would be far greater for the individual managers, than for the company itself. This explains their risk-averse attitude.

Managers in big companies are less comfortable with disruption

According to recent research by *Harvard Business Review* amongst executives from 3,000 companies worldwide, it appears that managers of mid-sized companies with revenues less than $1 billion a year are more comfortable with change and disruption than executives from bigger companies [2]. As you can see, more than half the executives are worried about losing their job due to the disruption facing their industry.

I worry about losing my job due to the disruption facing my industry.

51 per cent of the executives from companies
with revenues > $1 billion.

47 per cent of the executives from companies
with revenues $500 million – $1 billion.

30 per cent of the executives from companies
with revenues $100 million – $500 million.

Leaders of smaller companies feel they are better equipped to cope with disruption. Their teams are more agile, they worry less about their own jobs, they have a better handle on priorities, and their workforce is less likely to resist change.

Showcase innovation successes: A Harley-Davidson case

Given the risk-averse attitude of senior managers in your organisation, you can start winning their buy-in for change showcasing innovation in a couple of ways.

Suppose you just joined an American company called Harley-Davidson, as their new central innovation manager. It experienced a large growth with revenues of $5.8 billion in 2023, employing 6,400 people in a highly centralised organisation. Most of the company's stock is owned by institutional investors.

Harley-Davidson is struggling to maintain its dominance in the motorcycle market, and the last decade it failed to achieve its sales targets several times. In view of the sharp drop in sales figures, the management launched the 'More Roads to Harley-Davidson' programme in 2018. As one of the outcomes of this programme they launched LiveWire, the first e-bike from Harley-Davidson. Unfortunately, LiveWire flopped. The new model clearly failed to address the millennium market because of its premium price and was temporarily withdrawn from the market after technical difficulties. Consequently, Harley-Davidson spun off its innovative electric motorcycle division end 2022.

Meanwhile, Harley-Davidson has continued to stick with their old and bulky models. As a new central innovation manager, how can you showcase innovation successes to get management buy-in for change again? I have four suggestions.

1. Use the entrepreneural spirit of the origin. You could revive the original entrepreneural spirit by bringing Bill and Walter Harley and Arthur Davidson back to life with virtual reality. And use it to inspire the present executive management of seventeen people by asking them: "How would Bill, Walter and Arthur innovate Harley-Davidson right now?"

The Origin of Harley-Davidson Motorcycles [3]

Bill Harley was born in Milwaukee, Wisconsin, in 1880. He came from a working-class family who had just arrived in the USA from Manchester, England. When Bill was fifteen, he found a job as an apprentice at a small bicycle repair shop. He loved the outdoor life and had a talent for drawing and natural history.

Two years later he found an apprenticeship as a designer draftsman at a small steel factory. It was no coincidence that his school friend Arthur Davidson was working in the foundry as a model-maker. The Davidson family had moved there from Aberdeen, Scotland twenty years before. The Davidson's were true Scots.

Harley really loved trout fishing and every weekend they went fishing together at the numerous lakes in the Milwaukee area. Around that time, when they were still in their teens, a German who had previously worked in Paris showed up at their small factory, carrying the drawings of a Dion Gasoline engine.

1903
first proto type

First, they constructed an engine for their small fishing boat. In autumn 1900, they got the idea to put an engine on a bike. The bike frame, however, was too light. In the course of 1902, Arthur got his 26-year-old brother Walter involved, who already had worked for a number of railroad workshops. By spring 1903, they had the first prototype of their motorcycle ready. Their contraption managed to reach 23mph (37 kph), but it still needed extra pedaling on the hilly back roads of Milwaukee. Naturally, that was unacceptable.

Harley designed a new and heavier motorcycle. And Davidson's father, a carpenter, built a 10x14-foot shed in the backyard for the boys to work in their spare time. Bill Harley thought he lacked the proper professional technical training and enrolled into a technical college that autumn. Walter Davidson gave up his job in spring 1904 to dedicate himself full time to motorcycles.

1905	**5**	In 1904, they sold three motorcycles, all with a 50 per cent payment in advance. They needed the buyers' money to afford supplies for the bikes. In 1905 they brought out 5 motorcycles, 49 in 1906, and 152 in 1907. At that time, Arthur's oldest brother William had joined them as well.
1906	**49**	
1907	**152**	
1908	**456**	By 1908 they had 36 employees on their payroll and produced 456 machines. That year Walter won a spectacular motorcycle race with 84 racers at the starting line, representing 22 motorcycle companies. Walter got the record score and they saw their business take off.
Business take off		

2. Showcase innovation successes from your own past. The Sportster is the most popular Harley-Davidson and the best-selling Harley of all time. Continuously upgraded over the years, it became an icon in American motorcycle culture. Launched in 1957, the Sportster is one of the longest continuously produced motorcycles in the entire world. Showcase the why, the development and the launch of the Sportster to inspire the executive board for change.

3. Showcase innovation successes from other iconic brands in look-a-like sectors. Like Harley-Davidson, the Fiat 500 is also an iconic brand. It was launched in the same year as The Sportster: 1957. After fifty years, the Fiat 500 got a great make-over with the inflatable model and is recently also very successful as EV. Showcase the remake of Fiat 500 to inspire the board for change.

4. Showcase innovation successes from competitors. In the 1960s, Honda wanted to enter the USA motorcycle market. By accident, via lead users, Honda found a whole new market in North America: that of the off-road recreational motorbike, in which their 50cc Super Cub fit perfectly. Showcase their unusual approach of discovering new motorcycle segments to inspire your executive management.

How showcasing innovation successes helps to win buy-in for change
Showcasing successful innovation projects like above, especially when they provide data-driven quantitative proof of success, helps you to win buy-in for change in two ways.

1. Realising Tangible Results: Highlighting successful innovation cases, like the Sportster, Fiat 500, and Super Cub with concrete outcomes demonstrates the potential (financial) benefits of change, easing concerns about the risks involved.

2. Bigger Competitive Advantage: Illustrating how embracing innovation has enabled other organisations to gain a competitive edge, emphasises the negative consequences of doing nothing in a rapidly evolving market, creating urgency to innovate.

When you showcase innovation by storytelling, you capture everyone's attention. Adding a proven financial 'magic sauce' makes it even more convincing, breaking risk averse behaviour. In the next chapter I will present another great strategy to reduce risk aversion, by finding innovation partners.

Key messages from this chapter:

☞ When failing in innovation in a big company, your reputation or even your job is at risk.

☞ Leaders of smaller companies feel they are better equipped to cope with disruption.

☞ Highlighting successful innovations demonstrates the benefits of change, easing concerns about the risks involved.

☞ Showcasing innovation illustrates how embracing innovation has enabled other organisations to gain a competitive edge.

[1] *Harvard Business Review*. https://hbr.org/2020/03/your-company-is-too-risk-averse
[2] *Harvard Business Review*, https://hbr.org/2023/05/how-midsize-companies-can-make-the-most-of-disruption
[3] Marcel Grauls, *Het paard van Ferrari* (2003), Publisher Balans en Van Halewyck, Amsterdam

Nelson Mandela

Nelson Mandela

"It always impossible

seems
until it's
done."

10 Find Innovation Partners

IMPACTS MOST

1 HISTORICAL SUCCESSES

IMPACTS ALSO

2 LACK OF DIVERSITY

5 BUREAUCRACY

Looking back on historical innovation successes and the way we developed them is a barrier for innovation, especially when you need to innovate in a radically different way than in the past. Co-creating with innovation partners is a great way to get access to new insights, new strategies, new technologies, new markets, new ways of development, new ways of production or new ways to launch your new solutions. It also helps you to break the barriers of a lack of diversity and bureaucracy within your organisation, as you don't have to do everything yourself anymore.

Innovation partnerships accelerate innovation

Radical innovation is hardly a solo act anymore, especially in big companies. In the USA, UK and Germany, 95 per cent of the main companies practice open innovation. This is also increasing in small and medium-sized companies, which adopt it in 48 per cent of the cases, with peaks of 63 per cent for medium-sized enterprises [1].

Innovation partnerships offer many advantages. Accelerating innovation and commercialisation is the main reason why 94 per cent of tech industry executives consider innovation partnerships a necessary strategy [2]. You will have your personal experiences with open innovation too, I imagine.

A multiparty ecosystem innovation approach

You can identify and engage innovation partners per project on an ad hoc basis, as most organisations do. I'd like to highlight here a much more exciting approach for what is called multiparty ecosystem innovation. And share the CHILL example of Cisco engaging with Airbus, DHL, Caterpillar simultaneously to co-create groundbreaking new solutions.

- -

CHILL: Cisco Hyperinnovation Living Labs [3]

- -

At Cisco Hyperinnovation Living Labs (CHILL) in Berlin, innovation champions and senior executives of four large established companies: Airbus, DHL, Caterpillar, and Cisco, gathered to co-create breakthrough innovations.

The event, hosted by Cisco, the California-based networking and technology company, was a crucial point in a process designed to tackle the most pressing challenges at the intersection of supply chain and digitisation. The ambitious goal was to launch partnerships for groundbreaking solutions to shared problems within the next six months. CHILL differs from similar approaches, such as R&D alliances, because it focuses on the fast and agile commercialisation of ideas without a complicated intellectual property agreement.

Collaborating effectively with four partners at once, each one an enormous organisation with its own distinct culture and objectives is a massive challenge. The CHILL team coordinates the ecosystem and the application of tools and methods drawn from design thinking, lean start-up, and business model innovation methodologies. The process has four phases, which run over several months.

- -

1. Identify the 'focus zones' and innovation partners.
First, the host company, Cisco, identifies the arenas of opportunity, or focus zones, that are important to its own strategy. The CHILL team uses a scorecard to assess potential partners along three dimensions: maturity in innovation capability; a well-developed internal innovation process; and experience partnering with other companies, working with start-ups, or investing in start-ups. It selects partners based on alignment of goals, market power, and resources.

- -

2. Find and define the problem.
A successful ecosystem innovation effort includes a robust problem discovery and definition phase. CHILL team members spend three months preparing. They talk to dozens of ecosystem executives, along with experts, customers, and end users, to understand the real problems customers face and identify those that offer the biggest opportunities. After multiple rounds of conversations, the team eventually zeroes in on a single problem to be attacked. The final challenge statement (or 'ambition', as CHILL calls it) connects Cisco's strategy with those of its partners in the ecosystem.

- -

3. Gather the ecosystem to prototype solutions.
The most visible part of CHILL's ecosystem innovation process is the Living Lab, a two-day event that embraces a design thinking and lean start-up approach. At the core of that approach are rapid cycles wherein teams build a simple prototype, use it to test their 'leap of faith' assumptions with customers, and then apply the learning from that test to restart the build-test-learn loop.

As the second day of a Living Lab reaches its midpoint, the teams start to prepare their presentations for experts and investors – a panel composed of senior Cisco executives and executives from the participating organisations. The CHILL team brings in business analysts to help the teams think through the business model and the 'value at stake', a metric Cisco defines as value that could be created (new revenue) or costs that could be saved by the innovation.

4. Achieve commitment and follow-up.
After the teams present their innovations, executives who want to invest in one, including the panel 'judging' the event, must commit on the spot. The goal is to get an instant decision and 'timebox' the innovation cycle, which otherwise might run on and on. This also creates excitement that is vital to the future success of the project.

This ecosystem innovation process allows companies to bring extremely diverse ideas, skills, and resources together to solve ecosystem-level problems at astonishing speed. It also helps them build the innovation capabilities needed for a digital age and the collaboration skills to capture the valuable opportunities that sit at the intersection of products, companies, and industries.

Early results are impressive. For example, Cisco estimates that the Airbus-DHL-Caterpillar lab produced internal projects, spin-outs, and joint ventures to digitise supply chains, factories, and warehouses that will generate $6 billion in new revenue and save $3.4 billion in costs over the next 10 years.

This well-structured multiparty ecosystem innovation process allows companies to bring extremely diverse ideas, skills, and resources together to solve ecosystem-level problems at great speed, and generates impressive results.

Seven tips to manage relationships with innovation partners
Successful innovation partnerships must be well-managed to deliver mutual radical benefits. Finding the right innovation partner with matching cultures and complementary capabilities is quite a challenge, of course. When there's mutual trust, having a competent partner on board is a great way to help you to win buy-in for change with your own executives.
I have seven tips for you for managing the complex relation with your innovation partners:

1. Maintain transparent and open lines of communication.
2. Build trust by being reliable, honest, and by delivering.

3. Encourage collaboration by sharing ideas, insights and expertise.
4. Actively involve stakeholders throughout the process.
5. Reward by celebrating successes and publicly give credit where it is due.
6. Clearly define agreements and expectations regarding intellectual property rights.
7. Foster a learning culture by sharing, reflecting, and encourage experimentation.

Match risks with benefits

In innovation partnerships it is common to allocate risk by making each partner responsible for its own costs from the start of the project through production. But will that guarantee the best results? When you allow all innovation partners to take risks proportional to the potential benefits being offered to them, there's an incentive to get the best people on the job, where the stakes are the highest.

The crucial success factor is trust

In the end, all great innovation partnerships come down to trust. If you want to develop and commercialise radical innovations, you need to collaborate with partners based on clear win-win rules of engagement and allocate the risk fairly for all. If you can manage that, you'll be able not only to deliver but also to accelerate your innovation.

When done right, open innovation pays off

P&G, a leading consumer goods company, has been a pioneer in open innovation. Through its Connect + Develop programme, the company collaborates with universities, start-ups, research institutions and individuals to source innovative ideas and technologies. This programme has yielded numerous successful products, including Swiffer, Febreze, and Tide Pods. In 2021, P&G reported that 50 per cent of its innovations originated from external collaborations, showcasing the programme's effectiveness in fostering innovation and driving growth. When done right, open innovation pays off.

In the next chapter, I will present you Strategy 11: be customer-centred, which will be a real game changer to win buy-in for change.

Key messages from this chapter:

☞ Innovation partnerships accelerate innovation and commercialisation.

☞ A multiparty ecosystem innovation approach can deliver huge extra value for all partners.

☞ All great innovation partnerships come down to trust.

☞ When done right, open innovation pays off.

[1] The Innovation Barometer. The Economist Group 2022. 500 business executives in the USA, the UK and Germany.

[2] *Harvard Business Review*. https://hbr.org/2022/07/what-makes-innovation-partnerships-succeed

[3] 'Managing Multiparty Innovation.' *Harvard Business review*, November 2016, by Nathan Furr, Kate O'Keeffe, and Jeff Dyer. https://hbr.org/2016/11/managing-multiparty-innovation

Ryunosuko Satoro

"Individually drop, but we're an

we're one together ocean."

11 Be Customer-centred

IMPACTS MOST

1 HISTORICAL SUCCESSES

IMPACTS ALSO

12 NO PRIORITY TO INNOVATE

13 NO CLEAR DIRECTION TO INNOVATE

Making innovation customer-centred, breaks the barrier of a lack of market focus. It will also help you to get innovation on senior management's agenda, as it will boost customer satisfaction and consequently net promotors scores. Placing the customer at the core of your innovation initiative will inspire the team and give a clear direction too.

Relevant customer problems lead to great new solutions

In innovation you wow customers when you solve relevant problems for them. So that's where innovation starts for me, as well as for Melitta Bentz: identifying relevant needs, issues, challenges, problems, frictions, or dreams. When your innovation mission is solving a relevant problem in a new way, people will change their behaviour, and adopt your (radical) new solution. It provides a certain business model too, as your new offering adds real value. And this customer buy-in boosts management buy-in for innovation.

How an irritated Melitta invented the coffee filter [1]

Melitta Bentz would start out her mornings in Dresden with a cup of freshly brewed coffee. But rather than feeling refreshed and focused, Bentz found herself growing more annoyed with each sip.

"My mother, who had an excellent taste in coffee, was often irritated by the coffee grounds in her cup," recalled Horst Bentz, one of her sons.

And then there was the chore of cleaning the copper pot and getting rid of the grounds that stuck to the sides. Every morning, from her kitchen, Melitta fantasised about better ways to brew.

She tried and failed multiple times, until one day she ripped a piece of blotting paper from her son's school notebook and stuck it into an old tin pot in which she had punched some holes. What she did next will sound familiar to many: she added ground coffee and poured hot water over it. The beverage dripped through the paper, straight into the cup.

Cleaning up was easier and more hygienic; the used paper filter went straight into the trash, with no more handling of messy grounds.

In June 1908, The Imperial Patent Office in Berlin granted Bentz the patent for the paper filter. Today, the Melitta Group employs more than 6.000 people from all over the world and has a revenue of € 2.3 billion.

Delighting customers should be your mission

There's always a new way, also in your market. That's why Jeff Bezos is so right when he states that customers want something better, even when they don't know it yet. Standardising, digitalising, and improving the customer journey is a great start and leads to a better appreciation. But when was the last time you were wowed as a customer?

You can recall it exactly because it made impact. When your tailored innovation is creating a wow-experience for your customers, it generates a great buy-in from them. And this customer buy-in validates new business models and will help you to win buy-in for change.

Delighting customers as a mission [2]

Founder and former-CEO Jeff Bezos wrote once to his Amazon shareholders:

"Customers are always beautifully, wonderfully dissatisfied, even when they report being happy and business is great. Even when they don't yet know it, customers want something better, and your desire to delight customers will drive you to invent on their behalf."

Find new unmet needs by four ways of looking

Everyone works on better solutions for known issues from customers, who are well-aware of them. But as soon the new solutions pop up, the new markets will be crowded and turn into red oceans in no time. Innovation success is more sustainable when you create a radical new solution for an accepted customer pain, breaking old behavioural habits. Or you could even take it a step further and fulfil a customer dream by creating radical new solutions, driven by new technology that brings science fiction to life, with AI, virtual reality, or robotics for example.

Whichever innovation route you prefer, identifying unmet customer needs, pains or dreams are crucial. And you must interpret them right way to be able to ideate proper new solutions. To increase your chances of accurately detecting customers' problems and dreams, you must diversify how and where you look. That's why I introduce 'Four Ways of Looking', originally developed by Louis Barsoux, Michael Wade, and Cyril Bouquet. [3]

It involves two main approaches: improve your vision of mainstream users and challenge your vision by looking at unconventional users. Within each, you can adopt a narrow focus or take a wider view. You can zoom in on individual mainstream users and their everyday experiences (the microscope strategy). Or you can pull back to discover patterns in their aggregate behaviour (the panorama strategy). Similarly, you can take a close-up look at users outside your core (the telescope strategy). Or you can seek a broader view of their patterns as a group (the kaleidoscope strategy). Let's dig into it.

1. *The Microscope Strategy.* By zooming in on the experiences of your mainstream users you can identify unsurfaced needs through regular focus groups, interviews, or questionnaires. This is a natural starting point for many inventors, like Melitta Bentz, who discovered the coffee filter to address her personal frustration. You step into a role of an anthropologist to understand the passions, frustrations, needs, and wants of your users. They will serve as a solid base for radical new solutions that can support those needs and wants.

2. *The Panorama Strategy.* By this way of looking, you can find unmet needs of mainstream users by looking at aggregated data, such as errors, complaints, and accidents, that amplify weak signals. Digital tools make it much easier to observe the behaviour of large numbers of individuals. The 'big data' needed can be collected from multiple sources like apps and smartphones and can be analysed for trends.

When you keep looking at and interacting with the same mainstream customer groups, in the same context, with the same tools, you surely will miss new outside-the-box opportunities. That's why I like this model, as it forces you to look at unconventional users too.

3. *The Telescope Strategy*. With this strategy you study fringe users, extreme users, nonusers, or even misusers. Demands from small niches are often dismissed as irrelevant. But when you zoom in on users at the periphery, you might uncover pain points that are relevant to the masses too, especially when they are lead users.

4. *The Kaleidoscope Strategy*. You can also look at distant groups together and find similarities that show unmet needs. It's like spotting patterns in a kaleidoscope. The challenge, especially for managers in established companies, is to think beyond the usual groups like suppliers, distributors, and competitors. Make use of digital tools and AI to quickly analyse masses of data and identify patterns. Scrutinise user-generated content to capture insights at the 'user moments of experience' that shed light on users' emotional states along with specific malfunctions, difficulties, or missing features in the product or service at hand.

Four ways of looking

Challenge your vision by looking at unconventional users

Telescope Focus closely on users outside your core	**Kaleidoscope** Focus broadly on users outside your core
Microscope Focus closely on mainstream users	**Panorama** Focus broadly on mainstream users

Zoom in — Zoom out

Improve your vision of mainstream users

Source:
Louis Barsoux, Michael Wade,
and Cyril Bouquet

Being customer-centred will boost your innovation performance. This will be empowered by Strategy 12: Apply proven methodologies, as in most of them the voice of the customer is included.

Key messages from this chapter:

☞ Delighting customers should be your mission.

☞ Relevant customer problems lead to great new solutions.

☞ Innovation starts by identifying relevant needs, issues, challenges, problems, frictions, or dreams.

☞ Find new unmet needs by four ways of looking.

[1] New York Times, 2018/09/05. https://www.nytimes.com/2018/09/05/obituaries/melitta-bentz-overlooked.html
[2] 'How Corporate Purpose Leads to Innovation', HBR, November 01, 2023.
[3] 'Four Ways of Looking', Harvard Business Review, July-August 2022. Louis Barsoux, Michael Wade, and Cyril Bouquet https://hbr.org/2022/07/identifying-unmet-needs-in-a-digital-age

Gijs van Wulfen

"Customer management

buy-in boosts buy-in."

PROCESS-RELATED STRATEGY

12 Apply Proven Methodologies

IMPACTS MOST

1-4 NOT KNOWING HOW TO INNOVATE

IMPACTS ALSO

6 ORGANISA-TIONAL SILOS

7 RISK AVERSION

How long will it take to innovate? How can we generate concrete new outcomes? And will the new concepts generated be successful and have any impact?

You might have an answer to these questions, as innovation might be your daily business. For a lot of people and organisations, however, it's not. For them, one of the main barriers to innovate is that they just don't know how to it. They lack the knowledge and experience. That's when Strategy 12: Apply proven methodologies is of great value. Using a proven methodology creates confidence and trust among those who work with it, while also lowering the barrier of risk aversion. And as proven methodologies mostly involve diverse multifunctional teams, they will help you break organisational silos as well.

A proven methodology reduces uncertainty

First, your (client's) organisation might have little experience, and doesn't know how to innovate. This could be the case for non-profit or governmental organisations that never had to generate income and were completely financed by governments or financial benefactors. And this also counts for old family companies, where for decades the original products or services and all their adaptations created a prosperous future. It could even apply to scale-ups who became successful with the original concepts, launched a long time ago.

That's why applying a proven methodology makes a lot of sense, as it will reduce uncertainty. There are five compelling reasons why the use of a methodology can benefit your company's innovation efforts:

1. Structured approach: methodologies provide a systematic and structured approach to innovation, guiding teams through each step of the process from ideation to implementation. This helps prevent chaos and makes your efforts more effective.

2. Increased efficiency: by following a methodology, teams can streamline their innovation processes, reducing the time and resources required to bring new ideas to market. This ensures resources are allocated efficiently and you can respond to changing market demands more quickly. The rapid development of artificial intelligence will boost efficiency of proven methodologies enormously. Leading companies, such as GE and Nestlé, have showcased applications of AI in new product development with great effects. GE boasts a huge 50 per cent

reduction in development times, while Nestlé reports a dramatic 60 per cent increase in the pace of innovation. [1]

3. Risk mitigation: innovation methodologies often include risk assessment and mitigation tactics, helping companies identify potential pitfalls early in the innovation process. By addressing risks proactively, companies can minimise the impact of failures and make more informed decisions.

4. Enhanced collaboration: many methodologies emphasise cross-functional collaboration and communication, bringing together diverse perspectives and expertise within the organisation. This collaborative approach fosters creativity and innovation by leveraging the collective intelligence of the team.

5. Measurable results: using a methodology enables companies to set clear objectives and key performance indicators (KPIs) for their innovation initiatives. This allows them to track progress, measure success, and make data-driven decisions to optimise their innovation efforts over time.

Especially when you work in a corporate culture characterised by risk aversion and fear of failure, the risk mitigation effect of implementing a methodology will help you to drive growth and stay competitive in today's dynamic business landscape.

Fifty proven innovation-related methodologies and techniques

There are a lot of innovation-related methodologies and techniques around. An innovation technique refers to a specific approach used to generate ideas or solve problems creatively within the innovation process. On the other hand, an innovation methodology is a broader framework or systematic approach that guides the entire innovation process from ideation to implementation. For example, brainstorming is an innovation technique where individuals generate ideas in a group setting, while Design Thinking is an innovation methodology that provides a structured framework for problem-solving, emphasising empathy, ideation, and prototyping.

Analysis & framing:
1. Fishbone diagram (Ishikawa Diagram)
2. Five whys (Sakichi Toyda)
3. Morphological analysis (Fritz Zwicky)

4. Value stream mapping
5. Empathy mapping
6. Customer journey mapping
7. Jobs to be done (Tony Ulwick)
8. Innovation focus workshop (Gijs van Wulfen)

Ideation and creativity:
1. Brainstorming (Alex F. Osborn)
2. Mind mapping (Tony Buzan)
3. SCAMPER (Bob Eberle)
4. Six thinking hats (Edward de Bono)
5. Rolestorming (Rick Griggs)
6. Analogous inspiration
7. Storyboarding (Webb Smith)
8. Provocation techniques
9. Crowdsourcing ideas
10. Lightning decision jam (Jonathan Courtney)
11. Hackathons
12. Design thinking (Herbert A. Simon)
13. FORTH innovation method (Gijs van Wulfen)
14. TRIZ (Genrich Altshuller)

Prototyping and experimentation:
1. Pretotyping (Alberto Savoia)
2. Rapid prototyping
3. Minimum viable product (Frank Robinson)
4. A/B testing
5. Design sprints (Jake Knapp)
6. Pilot projects
7. Fail-fast approach
8. Wizard of Oz technique (Jeff Kelley)
9. Business model canvas (Osterwalder & Pigneur)
10. Value proposition canvas (Osterwalder & Pigneur)

Collaboration and engagement:
1. Cross-functional teams
2. Co-creation workshops
3. Open innovation platforms (Henry Chesbrough)
4. Nominal group technique

5. World café method (Juanita Brown and David Isaacs)
6. Participatory design
7. Innovation games
8. Communities of practice

Implementation and execution:
1. Agile methodology (Ken Schwaber and Jeff Sutherland)
2. Scrum framework (Ken Schwaber and Jeff Sutherland)
3. Kanban method (Taiichi Ohno)
4. Lean manufacturing (Henry Ford)
5. Stage-Gate process (Robert Cooper)
6. Waterfall methodology (Winston W. Royce)
7. Design for six sigma (Bill Smith)
8. Lean startup methodology (Eric Ries)
9. Continuous improvement (W. Edwards Deming)
10. Innovation metrics

Some of the 50 innovation-related methods and techniques mentioned above cover several stages of the innovation process.

As founder of innovation-related methods and techniques, like the FORTH innovation methodology or the Innovation Maze, I've experienced in practice the power of methodologies as they facilitate innovation teams by creating a shared learning process for team members. By these processes they create an open mind, and a greater awareness of the business, the market, the customers and even themselves. Sharing new insights, exchanging ideas, and co-creating together is at the core of a successful we-nnovation process. Also, as consultant, project leader and facilitator you benefit from using proven methodologies. They help to guide you, to keep the pace, and to monitor your progress on your innovation journey.

Below you can find ten techniques and methods, from each of the different categories, that I'd like to put in the spotlight, as they are proven ways to empower your innovation process.

The innovation focus workshop drafts a clear innovation assignment
As highlighted in Strategy 8: align innovation to strategy, the innovation focus workshop helps executives to transform a vague corporate strategy into a concrete innovation assignment. I have founded this technique as start of the FORTH

innovation methodology, to help organisations give innovation a clear direction. It's used even before the start of the innovation process itself to make clear what the desired outcomes of an innovation process should be. The innovation focus workshop involves five steps in which the main decision makers on innovation formulate the why, what, who, who, where and which for an upcoming strategic innovation project. The typical outcome is a straightforward innovation assignment containing also the criteria the new concepts must meet to be chosen for development and launch. The innovation assignment serves as a North Star for the innovation journey to come. The main takeaway of the innovation focus workshop is a clear understanding of the goals and deliverables of an innovation process by both the decisionmakers and the innovation team.

Customer journey mapping to understand the customer perspective

Customer journey mapping is a process of visualising and understanding the experiences a customer has when interacting with a business. This method is widely attributed to Lorraine Kettner, who introduced it in the 1990s. It's used at the start of innovation to identify pain points, opportunities, and areas for innovation in the customer experience. It's a valuable technique for when you improve products, services and customer experiences. The customer journey mapping process involves steps like research, persona development, mapping touchpoints, analysing emotions, identifying opportunities, and iterating on improvements. The outcome typically includes a visual representation of the customer journey, insights into customer needs, and actionable recommendations for enhancing the customer experience. Two main takeaways include a deeper understanding of customer perspectives and insights into areas for innovation with great potential.

Six Thinking Hats to consider different perspectives

The Six Thinking Hats method is a systematic approach to problem-solving and decision-making that involves wearing different 'hats' to consider various perspectives. The founder of the Six Thinking Hats methodology is Dr Edward de Bono, a renowned author in creative thinking and innovation. It's used to encourage critical thinking, collaboration, and holistic decision-making in situations where diverse viewpoints are beneficial. This might be brainstorming sessions or strategy meetings. The method works by assigning six different coloured hats to participants, each representing a specific mode of thinking (e.g., analytical, creative, emotional). It guides them to explore ideas from those perspectives in a structured manner. The outcome of the Six Thinking Hats method is well-rounded decisions, creative solutions, and improved communication amongst team members. The three main take-aways are a structured approach to decision-making, the promotion of diverse thinking styles, and enhanced problem-solving abilities within teams.

Lightning Decision Jam for fast-paced problem-solving in 90 minutes

The Lightning Decision Jam is a fast-paced approach to problem-solving and decision-making, inspired by design thinking principles. The founder of the Lightning Decision Jam is Jonathan Courtney. It's used to quickly generate ideas, evaluate options, and make decisions in time-constrained situations, such as product development or strategic planning. A typical Lightning Decision Jam is time-boxed and takes only between 30 and 90 minutes. It works by gathering a diverse group of stakeholders, defining the problem or decision to be made, ideating solutions, voting on the best options, and creating a plan for implementation. The outcome of the Lightning Decision Jam is rapid consensus-building, actionable decisions, and a clear path forward for innovation projects. The main take-aways are speed and efficiency in decision-making.

The FORTH innovation method to win management buy-in for innovation

The FORTH innovation methodology, as presented in Strategy 3: We-nnovate across silos, is a structured approach to innovation that focuses on finding, filtering, fast-tracking, and fostering innovative ideas for successful implementation. It combines Design Thinking and business thinking. FORTH is used when organisations want to systematically innovate by identifying promising ideas, refining them, and swiftly bringing them to market to stay ahead of competitors. It works by first drafting an innovation assignment and assembling a top team (Full Steam Ahead). Then you gather new insights through exploration (Observe & Learn). It's followed by generating new ideas and concepts (Raise ideas). Then you filter and select the most promising ones. And you fast-tracking their development through testing (Test Ideas). Finally, you foster their implementation and scale concepts by drafting new business cases at the enod of the innovation journey (Homecoming). The outcome of the FORTH innovation method is five new business cases for successful innovations, while sparking a culture for innovation. The three main take-aways are: a structured approach to start innovation, a focus on winning management buy-in for innovation, and a systematic way to foster a culture of innovation. It has proven to double the innovation effectiveness of stage-gate processes.

Pretotyping to fake it before you make it

Pretotyping is a way to test the feasibility and desirability of an idea quickly and cheaply before investing in full-scale development. The founder of the Pretotyping method is Alberto Savoia, a former Google executive and innovation expert. You

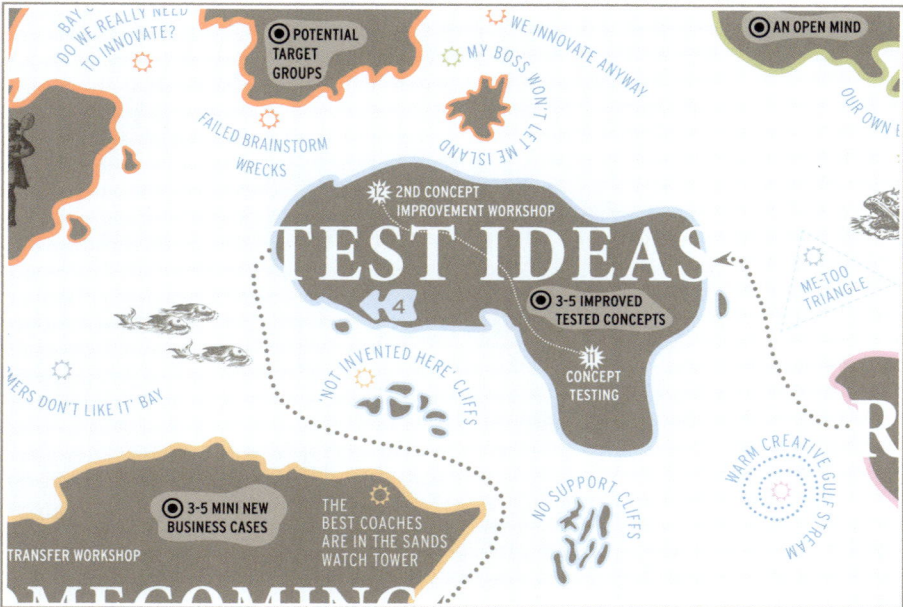

FORTH innovation method step 4: Test Ideas (see page 67).

can use it when you want to validate assumptions and test concepts early in the innovation process to minimise risks and optimise resource allocation. You first create rough low-fidelity prototypes that simulate the core functionality of an idea. Then you gather feedback from users or stakeholders, and iterate your concept based on the insights gained. The main benefit of the Pretotyping method is reduced time to market and cost savings by avoiding investment in ideas that are not viable or desirable. You focus on rapid experimentation and learning, as you fake it before you make it.

Design Sprints to validate solutions in a week

The 5-day design sprint is a structured process for rapidly solving big challenges and testing new ideas in just five days. The founder of the 5-day design sprint methodology is Jake Knapp, a former Google Ventures design partner. It's used when businesses need to quickly develop and test innovative solutions. For example, you can apply it for launching a new product, improving a user experience, or solving complex problems. It works by bringing together a diverse team, defining the challenge, generating ideas, sketching solutions, deciding on the best approach, prototyping, and testing with real users. The outcome of the 5-day design sprint is validated solutions, clear direction, and actionable next steps for further development or iteration. The three main take-aways are: problem-solving and decision-making in a week, user-centric design approach, and the ability to validate ideas early through prototyping and testing.

Open Innovation Platforms to co-create solutions and share knowledge

An open innovation platform is a collaborative approach to innovation that involves engaging external stakeholders, like customers, suppliers, and partners, to co-create new solutions and share knowledge. The concept of open innovation was popularised by Henry Chesbrough, a professor and researcher at the University of California. Open innovation platforms are used when organisations want to tap into external expertise, access new markets, and accelerate innovation by leveraging the collective intelligence of a broader network. It works by establishing an online platform or ecosystem where participants can submit ideas, collaborate on projects, access resources, and share insights. Companies can then evaluate and integrate the most promising ideas into their innovation processes. The outcome of running an open innovation platform is increased innovation capacity, enhanced agility, and access to a wider range of perspectives and resources. The main take-away is leveraging external expertise and resources.

Lean startup for rapid iteration

The Lean startup methodology is an approach to building and managing start-ups that prioritise rapid iteration, experimentation, and validated learning. The founder of the Lean startup methodology is Eric Ries, a Silicon Valley entrepreneur and author. It's used when new businesses want to reduce the risk of failure and efficiently develop products or services that meet customer needs in a dynamic market. It works by starting with a minimum viable product, testing assumptions through customer feedback, measuring results, and iterating based on what's learned. The outcome of the Lean startup method is faster product-market fit, reduced waste, and increased chances of building successful, scalable businesses. The three main take-aways are: prioritising customer feedback and learning, embracing experimentation and iteration, and focusing on delivering value efficiently.

The stage-gate methodology to manage innovation projects

The stage-gate method is a structured approach to managing innovation projects. It breaks them up into stages and implements gates for decision-making and progression. The founders of the stage-gate methodology are Scott J. Edgett and Robert G. Cooper. You use it when businesses want to efficiently manage the innovation process, reduce risks, and ensure alignment with strategic objectives. Stage-gate works by dividing the innovation process into stages, such as idea generation, feasibility analysis, development, testing, and launch, with gates between each stage where decisions are made to proceed, pivot, or stop the project. The outcome of the stage-gate methodology is improved project selection, resource allocation, and speed to market. The three main take-aways are: a structured approach to innovation management, better decision-making through gate reviews, and improved accountability and control over innovation projects.

Applying proven methodologies, like the ones mentioned above, have a great number of advantages, helping you to win management buy-in. When you start using them, be also aware of some pitfalls like being time-consuming, being perceived as bureaucratic hurdles, or leading to innovation fatigue causing decreased motivation. To help you to prevent the occurrence of negative side-effects, I'd like to end with ten tips to speed up innovation in your organisation when you are implementing a stage-gate innovation process.

Ten Concrete Tips to Speed Up Innovation in your stage-gated process

1. Make clear criteria to ensure that go-no-go decisions are based on specific metrics.
2. Limit the number of innovation gatekeepers involved in decision-making.
3. Minimise paperwork and documentation.
4. Empower cross-functional teams to make decisions and drive projects forward.
5. Enable parallel processing of activities whenever possible to reduce timelines.
6. Integrate agile methods accelerating project progress.
7. Review your innovation projects regularly to address issues promptly, avoiding delays.
8. Maintain flexibility in stage-gate criteria to adapt to the unique needs of each project.
9. Reallocate resources from low-potential projects to high-potential ones to maximise ROI and speed.
10. Refine your stage-gate process to streamline it over time.

By using the proven innovation methodologies above and implementing these tips, you can make your innovation process leaner and faster, enabling you to win management buy-in, and bring new ideas to market more efficiently and effectively.

Check out the next chapter on NTT DATA's choice for proven global innovation methods.

Key messages from this chapter

☞ There are proven innovation methods and techniques for every stage of the innovation process.

☞ Applying a proven method makes a lot of sense, as it will reduce uncertainty by addressing risks proactively.

☞ Proven methods enable organisations to set key innovation performance indicators (KPIs) to make data-driven decisions to win management buy-in for innovation.

[1] Cooper, Robert G. 2024. 'Unleashing the Power of Artificial Intelligence in New Product Development: Building AI Into Your Stage-Gate® New-Product Process', May 1. Article #6 at: Robert G. Cooper - Artificial Intelligence in NPD (bobcooper.ca)

Gijs van Wulfen

"On the vast ocean of innovation, your path is your power."

HOW PROVEN METHODOLOGIES HELP NTT DATA INNOVATE JAPAN

By Yuya Nishimura

NTT DATA is Japan's largest IT services company with the sixth largest market share in the world. In July 2023, NTT DATA transitioned to a holding company structure and spun off its operations into three separate companies. This is the Innovation Story of the NTT DATA Japanese subsidiary.

A LOT OF JAPANESE MANAGERS DON'T KNOW HOW TO HANDLE INNOVATION

As part of their corporate culture, Japanese people and companies are extremely fearful of taking on challenges that involve uncertainty and ambiguity. Especially in innovation and new business development, there is a tendency to extrapolate the present business thinking to the future. Due to a lack of understanding the mechanisms of new business development, top managers trust that assigning a leader to new business development who excels in the daily business will work out well. Furthermore, any new business idea or innovation proposal that goes hand in hand with challenging uncertainties, is stopped by senior management straight away. As a result, companies face a lot of issues when starting to innovate, for example: "We're not able to generate very innovative ideas", "We struggle with creating new concepts and how to verify them", and "Not many ideas and new concepts reach the launch stage".

That is why NTT DATA began to take on the challenge of becoming the innovation partner of choice for its customers in Japan. In the past, our added value was often limited to solemnly building and providing IT services based on customer requirements. Our customers had already engaged in workshops and brainstorms based on Design Thinking only, experiencing some success but also significant failures. And they were fed up with these failures. As we embarked on the challenge of co-creating new business ventures with our clients, we decided to start with one question:

"Why have we been approaching new business development, which inherently creates uncertainty, without setting any direction? And that while even waterfall-style system development requires a project charter?"

Furthermore, we conveyed the following to the decision-makers amongst our clients:

"We need direction. And we call that direction the innovation assignment. Let's establish the innovation assignment first. It's not just about brainstorming for now."

This message resonated strongly amongst our Japanese clients. It convinced them that our proposed approach to business development, starting from a fundamentally different perspective than the ineffective methods used before, was the way forward. And that created management buy-in to for change and started the new business development journey.

NTT DATA'S CHOICE FOR PROVEN GLOBAL METHODS

One of the factors enabling us to become the innovation partner for our clients, was selecting Design Thinking and innovation methodologies, which suited both us and our Japanese customers well.

In selecting innovation methodologies, we paid special attention to three important aspects:

1. It must have a clear structured process leading to concrete innovative outcomes.

2. It must be supported by an easy-to-use versatile toolkit which is simple to apply by both our NTT DATA consultants as by the participants from our clients.

3. It not only leads to concrete outcomes, but also facilitates creating a Design Thinking innovative mindset at participants.

Workshops based solely on several design approaches they had already undertaken lacked the realism to build business effectiveness, leaving them disappointed. Similarly, projects led solely by business thinking consultants failed to resonate because they lacked the infusion of their own ideas and didn't deliver replicable success. However, the FORTH innovation method offered both the reality of realisation and the capability for them to achieve replicable success. When choosing FORTH, clients didn't exercise their comparative rights with other methods.

As a result, NTT DATA has chosen to implement the FORTH innovation method, a globally

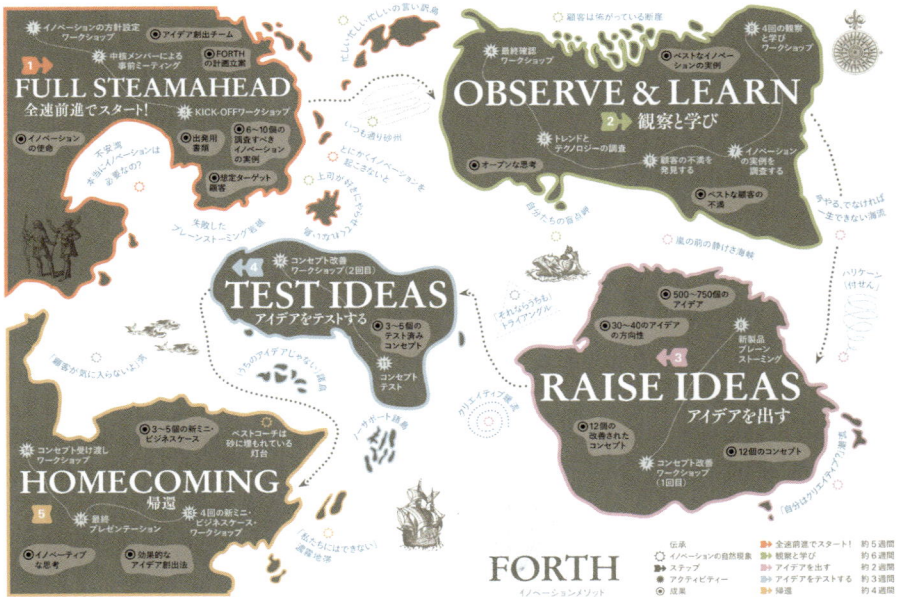

FORTH innovation method in Japanese (see page 67)

proven method to start innovation, as of 2021. This method matched all the requirements above and has proven itself to create excellent results in diverse industries and sectors, all over the world and in Japan since 2015. In that year, one of the books of Gijs van Wulfen was published in Japanese called *START INNOVATION! With this visual toolkit.*

At the start, however, due to the uncertainty avoidance, Japanese companies and professionals are reluctant to adopt things from abroad, no matter how well-established a method may be. We were aware of this risk and wanted to provide extra comprehensive support to be able to deal with the cultural barriers to innovation within Japanese companies.

That's where NTT DATA's proprietary Business Design Sprint (BDS) came in. The BDS is a 'drill for new business development', crafted in a remarkably simple manner. It consists of four questions, eight perspectives, and 27 key questions. By filling in these hypotheses, creating a pitch deck, and iterating through cycles of hypothesis validation, it's possible to materialise ideas into business concepts and evaluate the viability of those concepts. As a consequence, the uncertainty created by innovation was diminished radically, creating a great buy-in for change from the participating clients. Within a few years, the FORTH innovation methodology and the Business Design Sprint already had a positive impact, both internally and externally, which I'd like to highlight in the next paragraphs.

CO-CREATING NEW BUSINESS MODELS FOR ELECTRICAL VEHICLES

As a concrete example, I'd like to share how NTT DATA and a major Japanese automobile manufacturer implemented a co-creation project with the FORTH innovation method. As the electrical vehicles will skyrocket by the year 2040, the aim was creating new business models related to Electrical Vehicles. FORTH, in combination with the Business Design Sprint produced excellent results. The new business concepts created in this Electrical Vehicles project are still in development at this point.

The FORTH method has been used mostly to create innovations within one company. As we at NTT DATA are sharing this methodology with clients, a unique evolution has been brought about. Half of the core innovation team for this new business development project consisted of members from NTT DATA, and the other half from the automobile company. In this way, FORTH is used as a co-creation-method for business development, creating great management buy-in from the client as they are part of the team.

HELP TEAM MEMBERS LEARN NEW INNOVATION SKILLS

In some new business projects with clients, the skill sets and skill levels of the team members from the client are insufficient. We have solved that in two ways. First, we added some of our own NTT DATA accelerators to the team. They share the same level of enthusiasm as the client's business development team and are process experts. Second, we added some NTT DATA subject matter experts to the team when they added value from a content perspective.

At the start of the innovation journey, the team spirit and relations are still somewhat rigid because of the relationship between client and vendor. That completely changes by working intensely together, and at the end of the project, the team is transformed into a real team; a 'safe zone' where everyone can discuss ideas and concepts openly on the same level. Another advantage of co-creating is that so far in all the cases, the projects raised the level of the client's team business development capabilities by learning them new innovation skills during the journey.

DEMOCRATISING INNOVATION
The certainty and reproducibility that the two methodologies create for our clients, we call democratising innovation. It breaks the traditional belief that only a handful of geniuses can realise innovation or new business development. And instead, we foster a state where ordinary but passionately driven innovators within companies can achieve results and thrive. Through our process of innovation, people are also discovering their own unique perspectives, thoughts, and creative abilities that they were previously unaware of.

As a specific spin-off, we are promoting the use of FORTH and the Business Design Sprint beyond the field of business development. NTT DATA started to experiment innovating human resource development, such as new employee training and internship programmes, We created a Business Design Sprint FieldTrip, which combines the essence of the FORTH method and BDS. The one-day programme FORTH INNOVATION METHOD. And it became a hit in supporting ideas at large Japanese companies, with more than fifty projects completed since its development, two years ago.

AN INTERNAL INNOVATION ECOSYSTEM FOR INNOVATION FACILITATORS
Innovation and new business development tend to be overly focused on the success or failure of individual initiatives. And business developers tend to be too focused on their own business successes and not on the successes of their colleagues or the accumulation and flow of knowledge to our organisation. Successful business developers leave our new business development department and move to other business divisions within NTT DATA, hollowing out the knowledge of the organisation, and leaving us only with unexperienced junior developers. To break this vicious cycle, NTT DATA has worked to train a large number of certified facilitators of the FORTH innovation method. NTT Data in Japan has 15 FORTH certified facilitators.

Creating many expert-facilitators with a common innovation language within the organisation has several advantages: they help each other and utilise each other's know-how to further improve the reproducibility of our success. Having a team of innovation facilitators helps to ensure that business development projects can be stably organised at any time and at any stage without falling into a personal dependency, and to ensure that project management is always up to date. Specifically, regular meetings of certified

FORTH facilitators, known as 'FORTHers', were held to brush up the project instruction guide and toolkit, share know-how and tips based on their own experience, and create support tools. They even took the initiative to create tools to support their projects.

Other FORTH innovation facilitators and I are not isolated from the rest of the organisation and created a system allowing us to collaborate on each innovation project across organisational boundaries. We developed a way of working by which two or more facilitators are always available to facilitate business design projects with clients. Furthermore, each individual facilitator can support and observe projects on a part-time basis to further refine their own facilitation experience. FORTHers made training programmes that they can offer at any time to their clients, and they can serve as instructors to provide their innovation facilitating expertise to NTT DATA clients as needed. This active internal ecosystem of innovation facilitators is always striving to maintain and improve their skills to enhance the innovation value we provide to our clients.

So when you want to implement a new innovation methodology in your organisation, I'd like to share five tips:

1. Choose methods which have proven themselves.

2. A good method contains a clear process, practical tools and elements that transforming mindsets.

3. Don't work alone but work together with innovation ecosystem partners.

4. Learn from your own anti-patterns of the past.

5. Achieving reproducibility for success is paramount.

13 Prove Customer Commitment

IMPACTS MOST

3 FEAR OF FAILURE

IMPACTS ALSO

11 NO MARKET FOCUS

15 NO CLEAR INNOVATION ROI

Prove that customers are committed to adopt your innovative solutions confirms there's a good product-market fit. It wins buy-in for change as it reduces the fear of market failure. Furthermore, it contributes to the trustworthiness of the projected ROI in your innovation business case. Scientific research shows that involving customers in the ideation and launch stages of the new product development process improves new product financial performance, as it accelerates time to market, and creates a better product-market fit. [1]

Three ways to prove customers are committed

Resistance to change, risk aversion, fear of failure, no clear return on investment – all these barriers to innovation hinder you at moments of decision-making.

When you need approval to enter the next phase of the development process, and especially to launch a new concept, proof of customer commitment helps you to win buy-in for innovation. There are three ways to prove customers are supporting your innovation.

1. *Proof of a problem-solution fit*: You provide proof that the customer problem you are addressing is real and your new concept effectively solves it, for example by positive test results from customers engaged in the innovation process, like lead users or regular customers.
2. *Proof of product-market fit*: You validate that your product meets the needs of the market and is accepted by a significant number of customers. It's the bedrock of any new solution, as it indicates that your product has a viable market. This data-driven validation might be based on customer engagement from experiments during the development process.
3. *Proof of business model fit*: You ensure that your business model (the way you make money) is sustainable and scalable. This data-driven validation might be based on scale-up experiments or from soft launch.

Richard Aberman,
co-founder
WePay [2]

"You can't define Product-Market fit, but you know when you see it. There are no specific KPIs, but you feel it."

Product-market fit is achieved when you have solved a customer problem and successfully launched the product as a pilot on the market, generating continuous demand and customer satisfaction. High retention rates, a high customer life-time value, and a customer churn rate indicate a strong product-market fit. Additionally, a high NPS score can signal that customers not only like your product but would recommend it to others, further evidencing a good fit with the market.

Heat-testing: a new way of validating product market fit in the real world [3]

The issue with market research to validate new product attractiveness and revenue potential, is that none of it takes place in a real-life environment. In every case, consumers are aware that they are part of a research effort. What's missing are data and insights about actual behaviour.

A great new way to validate your product market fit is using online advertising as market research.

Responses to a digital ad – clicks, likes, email sign-ups – are more reliable indicators of purchase intent because they reflect how consumers behave when nobody's watching. Testing via advertising captures real-life data about how customers respond to new product concepts. It's called 'heat-testing' – finding the spark between a new offering and an audience that is the genesis of product-market fit.

There's one question everyone wants to answer before they launch a new product like this one: is someone going to buy this thing? Fortunately, ad platforms lend themselves to multivariate testing, making it straightforward to access data-backed insights quickly. Platforms like Facebook, Instagram, X, LinkedIn, and Google have instant access to millions of consumers who can be segmented into discrete audiences and targeted with multiple ads featuring a new product. Some ads will work, and some won't, providing data about where to iterate variables.

So how do you know if there is demand for your new concept? When a potential customer gives your company their email address for a new product that does not yet exist, you're onto something. In an era in which privacy is increasingly valued, email is currency. A high rate of email sign-ups might be the best possible validation of potential demand for a Minimum Loveable Product (MLP) without actually building the product.

Indicators to prove customer commitment

Proving customer commitment will have a strong influence on winning management buy-in to change. Ideally, it means that you measure criteria which reflect the three types of fit. Usually, it works best to combine both qualitative criteria from interviews, surveys or social media interactions and quantitative indicators. Of course, which indicators reflect success the best, depends on your sector or industry.

Indicators you might like to measure quantitatively to prove customer commitment are: willingness to pay, customer acquisition cost, conversion rate, number of new customers, net promoter score (NPS), customer retention rate, and lifetime customer value.

How Tesla used a Lotus Elise to prove customer commitment for their Roadster

---

An excellent example of validating the product-market fit to prove customer commitment for an early-stage-concept comes from Tesla Motors. [3]

At the start of their company, the founders of Tesla had an ambitious idea (an all-electric 2-door sports car) and a marketing challenge (Tesla was an unknown quantity as a carmaker). In order to validate their concept, checking a product-market fit, Tesla created a pretotype of what the car would look like. The base for the pretotype was a Lotus Elise, the car whose chassis technology was ultimately licensed – and heavily modified – by Tesla to provide the basis for the Roadster chassis. Lotus supplied Tesla with a 'glider' Elise – a car without a powertrain –, which was filled with models of key components like batteries and AC motors.

This was not a prototype, because the vehicle didn't function yet and with a (relatively) trivial investment, Tesla was able to show prospective buyers a very close proxy for the final design. As if this wasn't canny enough, Tesla also deployed a 'fake door technique' to further validate demand. Instead of asking customers whether they "Would buy a Roadster" if Tesla built it, they asked "Will you put down a $5,000 deposit to have it built to order?" This is a true revealed-preference test, from which Tesla secured several hundred deposits, a non-trivial result to reassure investors.

Of course, experimenting with Minimum Loveable Products to prove customer commitment, is also a great opportunity to test the financial and technical feasibility (proof of concept) of your new solution, as input for your innovation business case. Indicators you might like to include are prototype performance, scalability, technical challenges, and production costs.

Onboarding co-developing customers as proof of commitment

In a business-to-business context in supply chains with only a few players, validating product-market fit is extra crucial, as you have only a limited number of customers. Getting one of them as a 'co-developing customer' to onboard your product development process is also hard proof of customer commitment, as you are sharing the risk and costs. You de-risk your innovation project, which will please senior managers.

Proving customer commitment for your new concept is a great bedrock for making an excellent innovation business case, which I will present to you in the next chapter.

Key messages from this chapter:

☞ Involving customers accelerates time to market and creates a better product-market fit.

☞ Prove a problem-solution fit, a product market fit and a business model fit.

☞ Heat-testing is a great new way to validate product market fit.

☞ De-risk your innovation project by onboarding co-developing customers.

☞ Proving customer commitment is a great bedrock for an innovation business case.

[1] *Journal of Marketing,* October 2015, Woojung Chan & teve Taylor, 'The Effectiveness of Customer Participation in New Product Development: A Meta-Analysis'.
[2] https://penfriend.ai/blog/product-market-fit-for-startup-success
[3] https://hbr.org/2022/12/validating-product-market-fit-in-the-real-world
[4] pretotyping@work, Jeremy Clark, 2012, pp. 25 -26.

Gijs van Wulfen

"The best guarantee to win manage-ment buy-in for innovation is a launching customer."

1-4 Draft an Innovation Business Case

IMPACTS MOST

15 NO CLEAR INNOVATION ROI

- -

IMPACTS ALSO

7 RISK AVERSION

10 NOT FITTING MANAGERS' GOALS

A crucial strategy to win management buy-in from senior management is delivering an innovation business case that meets their expectations and conditions. Drafting an innovation business case will solve the issue of 'no clear innovation return-on-investment (ROI)'. It will also help you to reduce the level of risk aversion dramatically, and you will clarify how your innovation business case contributes to the goals of your senior management.

You need a convincing business case to get the development funded

Does a great idea automatically sell itself? I wish it would. Can a senior manager recognise the potential of a great idea? That's the question. You might have heard of the story of Kodak. A Kodak engineer, asked by his supervisor, invented the first digital camera. They combined a new semiconductor with a television and data cassette to take a 0.01-megapixel photo. It took Kodak 16 years to get a single dollar from the invention: a one-off sale of a spy camera after a request from the US government. Kodak ignored the new idea because it didn't play nicely with its existing beliefs. [1]

A recent study by Erik Larson, based on survey responses from attendees at the 2023 Consumer Goods and Marketing Summit, measured the effectiveness of innovation-related decisions and compared the results to broader business decision-making benchmarks. [2] According to the survey analysis, innovation decisions are 2.5 times more likely to fail than typical business decisions, with outcomes missing expectations 50 per cent of the time.

History has shown us that a lot of wise people haven't been able to recognise the potential of a great idea. Even when it's the top management of your company that asks you to be innovative and expects you to break patterns, it is still wise to keep in mind that they are as conservative as ever. So the question is, how will you be able to help your colleague, your top manager, your shareholder or your venture capitalist to support your idea and fund the development and execution of it? As you're proposing an innovation to them, you must be aware that these decision-makers who are assessing your new concept might know very little about the new target market, the new product and business model or the new technology. They would like as much tangible proof as they can get before deciding. If they haven't decided anything, they don't run any risk. Once they say yes, they will be in it up to their necks. Their most essential question is: why should I fund the development of this new innovation?

The enemy of creativity is inside your organisation: your C-suite

Jennifer Mueller of the University of San Diego,
Jeff Loewenstein of the University of Illinois at Urbana-Champaign,
and Jennifer Deal of the Center for Creative Leadership
studied a company that was considering dozens of new product ideas.

The researchers asked middle managers,
C-suite executives, idea generators, and other stakeholders
to rate each idea on its creativity, feasibility, and profitability.

Then they asked customers how desirable each idea was.

The team found that the customers wanted the most creative ideas, but not the
ideas that people in the firm thought would be most profitable or feasible. [3]

Jennifer Mueller states:
"We believe that the major reason why novelty and feasibility are thought to be
at odds, is that new ideas involve more unknowns. CEOs want to see metrics,
such as ROI, to determine the viability of ideas, but for the newest ideas, such
metrics are hard to produce, if not impossible.
If decision makers are more tolerant of uncertainty
– if they focus on the why or consider that there are many possible solutions –,
it may mitigate their tendency to reject creative ideas."

Your idea will be evaluated from five perspectives

In an innovation business case, it is your challenge to be convincing. The more
radical your innovation is, the bigger the challenge as there will be more
uncertainties. In the boardroom your idea will be evaluated from at least five
perspectives:
1. The Customer: will they buy it?

2. The Technology: can we deliver it?
3. The Business model: will it pay off?
4. The Risk: what do we risk? What if it's a failure? What if it's a huge success?
5. The Fit: Why should we do it? What's the strategic perspective?

When the front end of innovation is finished, a lot is still unknown. The figures in your business case will be estimations, extrapolations, best guesses and, I also hope some hard results from your experiments. It is the potential risk of failure that makes managers and investors so prudent. Gilbert and Eyring found it useful to think in three categories of risks starting up a new venture: deal-killer risks, path-dependent risks, and easy-win, high-ROI risks. [4] Deal-killer risks are uncertainties that, if left unresolved, could undermine the entire venture. When you fail to spot a deal-killer risk, your innovation is doomed, so it's of extreme importance to identify and address the most important uncertainties in your innovation business case.

A practical framework for your innovation business case

For more than 20 years, I have been using and giving instructions on a handy, practical framework for an innovation business case. My advice is to just use PowerPoint (or keynote) instead of writing a full written report, as nobody will read it anyway. But of course, you must comply to the company guidelines. Here's the framework of a 9-paged innovation business case, which you can present in 20 minutes at the most.

Slide 1. Why?
☞ Why do I stick out my neck?
☞ Why should we stick out our neck?
☞ Why should our organisation stick out its neck?

Slide 2. The Customer Challenge.
☞ The customer's situation.
☞ The customer's needs.
☞ The customer's problem/challenge.

Slide 3. Our New Concept.
☞ The customer target group (qualitative and quantitative).
☞ The marketing mix of the new product, service, or business model.
☞ New for... (the world, the market, our company).

Slide 4. This Makes our Concept Unique.

☛ Buying arguments for the customer.
☛ Current solutions and competitors.
☛ Our positioning.

Slide 5. It will be Feasible.
☛ We can develop it.
☛ We can produce it.
☛ The development process.
☛ Our innovation delivery partners.
☛ Is it patentable?

Slide 6. What's in it for us.
☛ The number of customers (year one to three, or longer).
☛ The projected revenues (year one to three, or longer).
☛ The projected profits (year one to three, or longer).
☛ Other beneficial impact?.

Slide 7. Why now?
☛ Why to develop it now.
☛ What if we say no?

Slide 8. The Decision to Proceed.
☛ The major uncertainties.
☛ The development team,
☛ The process, costs, and planning.

Slide 9. Why We should Say Yes
☛ Why would I say yes?
☛ Why should you say yes?
☛ Why should the organisation say yes?

By making an innovation business case according to this format, you strengthen the persuasiveness of your proposal. It increases the chance you will get a yes, especially if you also have results from experiments done, and a pretotype or prototype which makes your new concept tangible and easy to understand.

As you are at the end of the front end, so entering the official innovation funnel, it will increase your trustworthiness when you make the uncertainties very explicit. In the innovation delivery process, there are plenty of possibilities to eliminate them.

To get a yes on your innovation business case, check out strategy fifteen on how to pitch your innovation story. But first read the incredible Innovation Story of how Bruil, a Dutch medium-sized concrete company, developed a radical way of 3D printing architectonical concrete.

Key messages from this chapter

☞ A lot of wise people haven't been able to recognise the potential of a great idea.

☞ You need a convincing innovation business case to get the development of your new offering funded.

☞ Your idea will be evaluated from at least five perspectives.

☞ The more radical your innovation is, the bigger the challenge to convince, as there will be more uncertainties.

[1] Max McKeown, *The Innovation Book,* Pearson, Harlow, United Kingdom, 2014, p. 24
[2] *Forbes*, https://www.forbes.com/sites/eriklarson/2023/10/25/five-reasons-why-innovation-decisions-succeed-25x-more-often-at-top-companies/
[3] Jennifer Mueller, *Harvard Business Review,* July 2014.
[4] Jennifer Mueller, *Harvard Business Review,* July 2014.

Jeff Bezos

"You cannot
business case
be who you

make a
that you should
are not."

THE INNOVATION JOURNEY OF BRUIL TOWARDS THE LARGEST 3D PRINTED CONCRETE PROJECT IN THE WORLD

By Theo Voogd

A world-wide deep crisis created an urgency to innovate

In 2012, the Dutch construction sector was hit by a deep crisis. As a result of the global financial crisis, the order book of almost all construction companies dried up. Hardly any new construction project was started. At a staggering pace, the total market volume halved.

At Bruil, as a supplier of concrete products, we were also hit hard by this crisis. Within a year our revenues halved. To keep our factories working, products were sold at increasingly lower margins. Ultimately, we had no choice but to sell products at or below our cost price. To stay afloat, we had to lay off one hundred of four hundred employees. Colleagues who had worked for us for decades lost their jobs. This had a huge impact on the Bruil family business, which revolves around loyalty and mutual trust.

After a year of reorganisation, an empty war chest and no sight of an end to the construction crisis, we worked to limit losses. Everyone feared for their jobs. When this situation stabilised somewhat, there was time to think about the future and discuss the questions that arose with each other: how is it possible that we, as a solid family business, are so vulnerable in times of crisis? How can we offer our colleagues hope and faith again? We get up every day not to lose, but how can we play to win again?

During this phase we learned that our product portfolio mainly consisted of construction products, which are proverbially available on every street corner; products that are made in large volumes at low margins. Often produced according to a rigid standard, so that there is hardly any distinctive character. If the market is stable, this is not a problem. But under pressure from the shrinking market, all producers want to continue working and see no other option than to lower the price.

We also noticed that different laws apply in times of crisis. Loyal customers are also having difficulty to survive. So they are more receptive to new suppliers. 'Long customer relationships' and 'added value' suddenly no longer count anymore. In short, we had to join the battle for the customer and implement price reductions. So we were well aware of the need for new products and services that would make us more resilient in the next crisis.

There are two ways to escape this situation: specialise or innovate. This is where the seed was planted at Bruil to start working on innovation on a structural basis. But how do you approach this in an organisation where there is no innovation culture at all? We found the answer in the FORTH innovation method, which allowed us to make a flying start with innovation.

THE DECISION TO INNOVATE

The decision to innovate structurally showed a lot of courage. In retrospect, it turned out to be the crucial factor in the transition from uncertainty to hope and perspective. During the FORTH innovation process, fifteen colleagues were partially released to work together on a new future. All other colleagues did their part by covering this temporary absence together and continuing their daily work. Within five months we transformed from a company with the intention of innovating to six broadly supported new business cases, which we started working on immediately. We played to win again.

During the start of the FORTH innovation process, a strategic departure document is drawn up. One of the questions is whether you are looking for 'evolutionary or revolutionary innovations'. Bruil decided to develop both evolutionary and revolutionary innovations. With evolutionary innovations, the result is more conceivable, but the impact is smaller. With revolutionary innovations, the result is less predictable, but the impact is greater. In other words: high risk, high reward. The decision to also want to develop revolutionary innovations is monitored at the various selection points in the FORTH innovation process.

During the discovery phase we came across a small article in a magazine. A University in California conducted research into 3D concrete printing. A robot stacked thin layers of concrete on top of each other to create a wall. There was hardly anything else to be found about it on the internet, but it immediately appealed to several problems that we and our customers experienced with prefabricated concrete products.

Bruil normally makes prefab concrete products in moulds. But these handmade moulds are expensive to make and are only used once or a few times. Besides that, it is non-recyclable waste. Moreover, the carpenters who can make these moulds are hard to find. The only way to produce affordably was to frequently reuse a mould. But this led to a lot of uniformity in architecture. 3D concrete printing could solve multiple frictions at once. Our interest was aroused, but the specialists among us had thousands of practical questions that could not be answered simply. During the assessment, this concept received a very high score for 'attractiveness', but also a very low score for 'feasibility'. A clear case of a revolutionary innovation.

AN EXPERIMENTAL BUSINESS CASE: WE'LL SEE WHERE WE'LL END UP

The innovation assignment to also deliver at least one revolutionary business case kept the 3D concrete printing concept on the table. We had to show courage and collect examples of successful 'moonshots' from history which were cited also to be impossible, but ultimately brought about a revolution. This 3D concrete printing concept could be a game changer for Bruil and our industry. But for management to opt for this innovation, a sound business case had to be made that met the criteria in the innovation assignment made at the start of our journey. We tested the concept at potential customers and made estimates of potential revenues after five years, and the investments needed. Step by step we worked out a pretty vague concept into a real business case. But how do you convince each other to decide to implement a revolutionary new business case?

Step by step, the assumptions that still caused much uncertainty were further investigated and verified. The uncertainty of a revolutionary business case was not hidden. The directors are experienced entrepreneurs who are well able to assess the risks. Quotes from customers helped to explain the need and customer issue in the market. And customer reactions from the concept test provided a positive insight that our revolutionary concept was able to solve them.

Finally, it helps to work in small manageable iterations. At the start of a revolutionary business case, it is impossible to draw up a balanced multi-year investment budget or to provide a conclusive answer to all technical questions in advance. You must start and start building to discover where the real bottlenecks are. After all, you don't know which persistent problems you have to overcome to be successful. We chose to formulate an objective for the first six months and submit a budget to the management. Six months is a manageable period for which it is easy to estimate what you can achieve. In addition, we have formulated milestones for the next two years, so that it is clear what the development should lead to. After every six months there was a go-no-go for the next phase. After those six months you will have a much better insight into the work and costs that will be required in the second half of the year. And so on.

FROM RADICAL NEW BUSINESS CASE TO A START-UP SETTING

The radical new business case '3D concrete printing of architectural concrete' was chosen by Bruil to develop, in addition to three evolutionary innovations. Once started, we managed to make the first 3D concrete prints within three months with a small team in an old workshop. Within six months we were able to show the first large-format concrete prints to the general public at a trade fair. This put Bruil on the map as an innovative company. This had enormous appeal to customers and suppliers. As companies like to work with other innovative companies, this has real 'added value' for the sale of our commodity products too.

Another unexpected side effect was that communication about these innovations led to many new requests and initiatives. We were, as it were, overwhelmed by a large number of innovative ideas and initiatives. From our customers, suppliers, but also from colleagues. That is why we decided to focus more on the direction in which we wanted to develop ourselves. This was recorded in a new mission and vision for our company.

Using the FORTH innovation method, we and a broad group of employees from the organisation researched the most important trends and developments in the market and the world. We selected the trends and new developments that influenced our customers and our work. We ultimately opted for far-reaching digitalisation (smart) and for reducing raw material use (circular and less); 'Making smart building products with less material'. These two spearheads are used to this day in our policy formulation and implementation.

A LAUNCHING CUSTOMER INITIATES A COMPLETELY NEW FACTORY

In the meantime, the 3D printing technology was further developed and the first discussions with launching customers were initiated. We made several demonstrators to show the progress and possibilities of the technology. Two and a half years after the first 3D print, a great opportunity presented itself. A well-known architect included 3D concrete printing in his design for the renovation of a gallery apartment from the 1970s. The design would transform the dated apartment building of 70 homes into a modern building, with a nod to the architecture of Antoni Gaudí. The wavy balustrades gave a Mediterranean touch to Den Helder, a city in the Netherlands. The new facade of the apartment building would be constructed from more than 700 3D-printed concrete elements, exactly as described in the original mini new business case. This opportunity marked a new phase for the project. It was necessary to scale up from a test location to an initial factory setup. The plan for a first 3D printing production location, until then still a visionary picture, was developed and Bruil Prefab Printing was founded.

THE LARGEST 3D PRINTED CONCRETE PROJECT IN THE WORLD

This meant scaling up the project with a major impact and a large increase in investment costs. The first assignment was realised through trial and error, which was the largest 3D printed project in the world until then. The process innovation involved in this fully digitalised factory turned out to be a much greater challenge than the development of 3D printing technology. There is a good reason for a well-known statement by Elon Musk: "It's relatively easy to make a prototype but extremely difficult to mass manufacture a vehicle reliably at scale. For cars it's maybe 100 times harder to design the manufacturing system than the car itself." This also applies to the 3D printing factory. A second flat is now also being renovated with 3D printed concrete elements, whereby the production process has come to fruition.

We would never have been able to develop all of this without a large group of brave people who, for better or worse, have committed themselves in recent years to the creation of Bruil Prefab Printing and the Baskeweg Project in Den Helder. It shows courage, entrepreneurship, and perseverance to make this radical development possible. This applies to the entrepreneurs: Hans and Dirk Jan Bruil, the employees of Bruil, Kokon Architectuur and Stedebouw, and not to mention our innovative customer Helder Vastgoed.

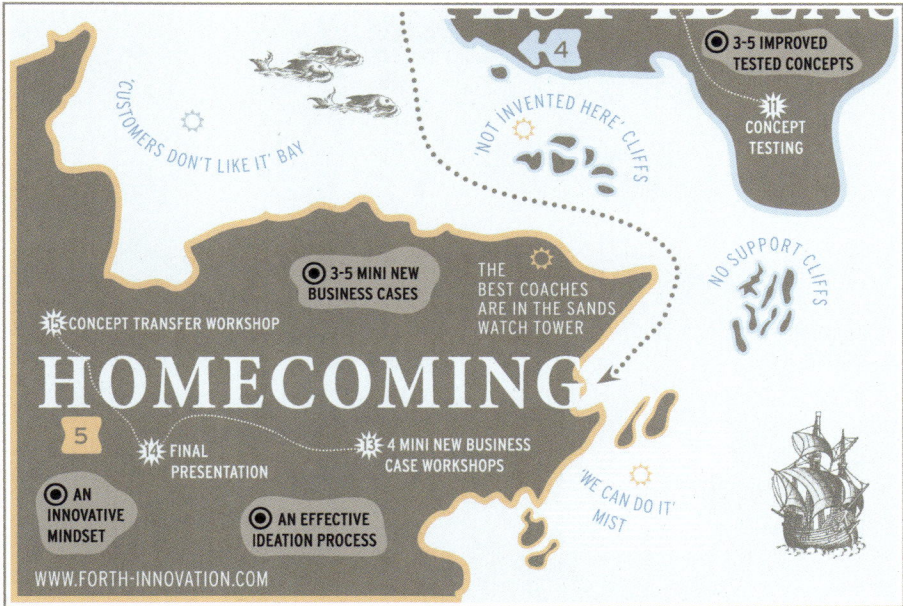

FORTH innovation method step 5: Homecoming (see page 67).

15 Pitch your Innovation Story

IMPACTS MOST

8 RESISTANCE TO CHANGE

IMPACTS ALSO

1 HISTORICAL SUCCESSES

9 SHORT-TERM FOCUS

A great story resonates. And that's why it gets you buy-in for change. It will open the eyes of those being imprisoned in historical successes, or the business of today.

I have seen a lot of innovative people presenting ideas in very original ways. By showing a movie. Doing a dance. Making a painting. Writing on one huge Post-it note. Making a newspaper. And even by doing a flashmob. Although it's very creative, the essence of presenting is to get approval from deciders so you can start a culture for innovation, and to proceed to the development phase or launch a concept on the market.

Four elements of a great story that drives radical business change

That's why I advise you to first craft an effective innovation story before trying to be original. I found four elements that will help you to tell a great innovation story that will help you win buy-in for change: understand your story in such a way that you can describe it in simple terms; honour the past; articulate a mandate for change; and lay out a rigorous and optimistic path forward.

Four elements of a great story that drives radical business change [1]

I love to share four key steps, developed by Frances X. Frei and Anne Morris that will help you to tell a story that will drive change in your organisation.

1. Understand Deeply, Describe Simply

This is the foundation of persuasive communication. When you think about the change you want to lead, ask yourself: can I capture my innovation vision in one page? One paragraph? One word?

2. Honour Your Past

Your next step towards creating the future is to revisit the past. First acknowledge the good parts of your history. To get everyone on board with your ideas, you need to show that you truly understand the organisation, starting with the good stuff. Then you reckon with the not-so-good parts. If your innovation initiative is to capture managers' hearts and minds, you'll need to confront your organisation's history with both optimism and honesty.

3. Provide a Clear and Compelling Mandate for Change

Now that you've honoured the past – the good, the bad, and the ugly –, it's time to share your rationale for creating a culture for innovation or launching new innovation projects. Begin by reflecting on the why of your plan. What problem are you trying to solve? Be persuasive enough to override the comfort of familiar beliefs and behaviours.

4. Describe a Rigorous and Optimistic Way Forward
Your next step is to get into the details of your innovation story. Why this new concept? How confident are you that it's going to be a success? In addressing those questions, you want to convey two things: rigor and – again – optimism. Let data help you demonstrate the first. Optimism is infectious and is one of your most effective tools.

You, as innovator, tend to think more radical. Be aware though that your senior managers will be as risk-averse as always and incorporate in your innovation story all the effective strategies presented in this book to win buy-in for change. So tailor your story to really fit your managers and their agendas (Strategy 1). And be sure it's explicitly aligned with your organisation's strategy (Strategy 8). Reduce risks by partnering (Strategy 10). Put the customer central (Strategy 11). Prove customer commitment (Strategy 13) and present a sustainable viable business case (Strategy 14).

The innovator's journey
You probably know 'the hero's journey', a widely recognised storytelling pattern that has been used for centuries in mythology, literature, theatre and movies. It's a framework that helps writers create compelling stories that resonate with their readers by depicting a protagonist who goes through a transformative journey. The journey usually involves a series of challenges that the protagonist must overcome to achieve their goal.

I have transformed the hero's journey to innovation, by converting it into a tailor-made outline for your story as innovator in twelve steps. You can use this outline for multiple purposes, for example:

1. To win buy-in to start creating a culture for innovation.
2. To win buy-in to start a specific strategic innovation challenge.
3. To win buy-in to launch a new product on the market.

Twelve steps of the innovator's journey

1. The call for radical innovation
This is the moment when the innovator receives a call to innovate, which could come in the form of a critical message of a customer, a nightmare of the company, running out of funds, or an encounter with a trendwatcher.

2. The refusal of the call for radical innovation. At this stage, the innovator initially refuses the call to adventure, due to fear of the internal resistance, doubt, and a sense of inadequacy.

3. Meeting the innovation ambassador. The hero encounters by coincidence a high-ranked innovation ambassador in his company who, after listening to his call to innovate promises leadership support, and guidance on the launch journey ahead.

4. Crossing the inside-the-box threshold. The innovator leaves behind the known world and crosses the threshold to the outside-the-box zone, getting new insights, and generating radical new ideas along the way.

5. Innovation tests, allies, and enemies. The innovator must navigate a series of tests, gates, and challenges, often with the help of internal innovation allies and the opposition of stage-gate steering committees.

6. The approach to the CFO. The innovator approaches the CFO for financial approval to launch, facing great fears and challenges.

7. The business case hell on earth. This is the moment of the innovator's greatest challenge, where they face approval of an innovation business case to continue to the launch.

8. The launching customer reward. The innovator achieves a reward – a deal with a launching customer to adopt the radical innovation – that helps them on their journey to launch.

9. The feasibility disasters. The innovator encounters after approval with feasibility disasters and cost price obstacles along the way.

10. The return from the feasibility death. The innovator experiences a moment of feasibility death and rebirth, when the last pilot production of the radical innovation succeeds for the first time.

11. Back to business. The innovator returns to his original department, transformed and changed by their innovation experiences, armed with new technological and marketing knowledge and customer insights that they can use to benefit the organisation.

12. The culture for innovation
The innovator achieves a state of
innovative mindset, coaching and
mentoring new innovation champions
on their exciting journies, being the
godfather of the radical innovation
that saved the company.

The twelve steps of the innovator's journey provide you with a roadmap for writing
a powerful innovation story that senior managers can relate to across cultures all
over the world. This innovation story outline for launching a new radical innovation
brings you at the end of the journey of this book too.

I wish and trust the the fifteen strategies I provided you with, helped you break the
wall of barriers to innovation at your (client's) organisation. And turned a lot of
those resounding nos into resounding yesses. Wishing you lots of success on your
path to becoming an amazing innovator, transforming your new ideas into reality
with impact.

Key messages from this chapter:

☞ A great story resonates, and gets you buy-in for change.

☞ Understand your story so well that you can describe it in simple terms.

☞ Honour the past and articulate a mandate for change.

☞ Lay out a rigorous and optimistic path forward.

☞ Use the storyline for the innovator's journey as your guide.

[1] *Harvard Business Review*, November-
December 2023. Frances X. Frei, Anne Morris.
https://hbr.org/2023/11/storytelling-that-drives-
bold-change

Gijs van Wulfen

"Successful innovators connect the past with the future."

Other Innovation Bestsellers

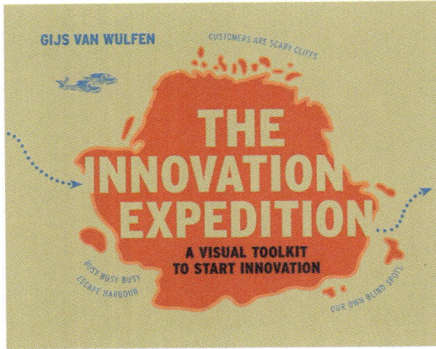

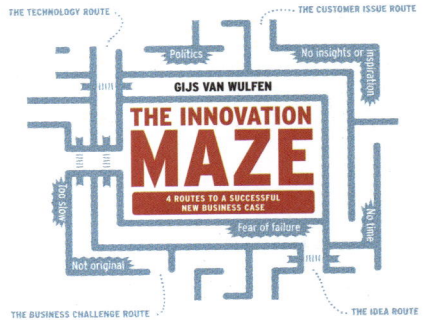

The Innovation Expedition

In this innovation bestseller *The Innovation Expedition*, Gijs van Wulfen shared his proven FORTH innovation methodology. It's used all over the world and doubles your innovation effectiveness, combining Design Thinking and business thinking. It inspires managers, consultants, entrepreneurs, and students with 240 pages full of exploration stories, quotes, charts, cases, checklists, formats, and innovation maps.

The Innovation Maze

The award-winning *The Innovation Maze* is a practical guide on how to navigate the innovation maze. It shows four clear routes and guides you through overcoming the obstacles to successfully deliver new business cases for products, services, and business models. *The Innovation Maze* makes innovation simple, delivering a coherent approach to the creation of new business cases. Written for start-ups, entrepreneurs, managers, and consultants.

Inspiration for Innovation

Inspiration for Innovation helps you to become a successful innovator. It offers practical insights, tips and tools and teaches you how to innovate. With 101 columns, it reveals how to achieve a strategic mindset: timing, breaking patterns, understanding customers, creating a culture for innovation, and implementing innovation projects successfully. The 101 lessons in this book make you dream, think and act like a successful innovator.

Online innovation

Hybrid innovation, combining in-person and online workshops using all the online advantages while being personally engaged offline, is here to stay. The authors (Maria Vittoria Colucci, Andrew Constable, Florian Hameister, Rody Vonk and Gijs van Wulfen) present ten methodologies, and 25 tools, helping you to pick the right ones for your online or hybrid innovation journey. This book supports all professionals who want to innovate the hybrid way: consultants, coaches, facilitators, managers, and students in Design (Thinking) and Innovation.

Index